The "Falling Away"

A biblical prophecy that the world is currently experiencing

Why is disobedience, divisiveness leading to wars, and lack of prosperity increasing throughout the world?

The stage is being set for the coming of a world-wide leader, the "Son of Satan"

The "Falling Away"

Table of Contents

The "Falling Away"

ACKNOWLEDGEMENT

I acknowledge and thank the "Holy Spirit" for inspiring me to write this book. I pray that it will answer many questions you may have pertaining to what's happening throughout the world today. To those who are snared by some of the characteristics of the "Falling Away," I pray that this book will enlighten you about the truth and that you will call upon Jesus Christ, our Savior, for deliverance.

<u>John 16</u>: "[7]Nevertheless, I tell you the truth; it is expedient for you that I go away: for if I go not away, the Comforter (Holy Spirit) will not come unto you; but if I depart, I will send him unto you. [8]And when he is come, he will reprove the world of sin, and of righteousness, and of judgment: [9]Of sin, because they believe not on me; <u>[10]Of righteousness, because I go to my Father, and ye see me no more;</u> [14] He shall glorify me: for he shall receive of mine, and shall show it unto you."

SPECIAL THANKS

TO:

Roberta L. Perkins, my sister in Christ, for her assistance and encouragement.

* * *

John Rosati, my brother in Christ, for his encouragement.

The "Falling Away"

Introduction

My name is Theresa Fuller, and the Holy Spirit has been an inspiration in my life for many years. He has inspired me to do numerous deeds that I would not have considered such as writing this book. When God first spoke to me in thoughts, I told myself that it was not Him. Writing a book was not something that I wanted to do, nor did I know what to write. After battling with the idea for months, God spoke to me again and told me to write about the **"Falling Away."** This time, my spirit was receptive, and I became enthusiastic about it. As a matter of fact, I began to realize that for years, God had been preparing me to write this book.

During the past two decades, I have observed a phenomenal increase and acceptance of disobedience against God's word among mankind, the law- makers, and the church. In questioning God about these observations, He empowered my spirit with an in-depth spiritual discernment of what's taking place throughout the world. There's a satanic spiritual warfare destructively progressing against mankind (Ephesians 6:11). This warfare is causing an increase of evil disobedience against the word of God to prevail; and it is causing world-wide destruction. Those who are disconnected from God cannot discern the current conditions nor do they understand what is actually happening. These things can only be discerned by the Holy Spirit.

The "Falling Away"

Today, the subtle movements of increased evil are in full bloom, and it's referred to in biblical scriptures as the **"Falling Away."** Wherever you go, evidence of it is staring you directly in the face. Those who are walking in darkness or disobedience to God's word are spiritually blind and deaf to the evil forces that exist. The majority of us believe that politicians are responsible for all that is going wrong in this world.

God does not discriminate. He warns both, Christians and sinners when a prophetic event is taking place or is on the way. He gave Noah a message to warn all of the people that a flood was going to take place that would destroy everyone throughout the world. They thought Noah was crazy, and his family had some doubt. The flood came with the destructive impact that Noah had prophesied. God has always used ordinary people to do extraordinary things. He gave me a message to write this book to warn people that we're living in the climax of a critical time known as the **"Falling Away,"** a dangerous time that is preparing the stage for the coming of the **"Son of Satan" also known as the "Antichrist."**

Many readers will disagree with the truths that are written in this book because of their lack of knowledge and spiritual separation from God. Some readers will recognize themselves in the depicted lifestyles of darkness and will turn away from destructive behaviors by seeking the ways of God. I have all confidence that since God is the co-author of

The "Falling Away"

this book, it will touch the lives of many who have not accepted Jesus Christ as their Savior and others who have been deceived by Satan to believe they're right with God when they're not.

Satan knows that he's running out of time and is busy deceiving and winning over as many as possible. The pathway to eternal damnation is becoming broader. He has influenced the majority to believe that he's a myth to prevent resistance. Know that Satan is alive and well. He has attempted to take my life on several occasions to prevent God's will for me to manifest. The victory was and is mine because God has a hedge of protection around me. **(Isaiah 54:17)**

The "Falling Away"

Prelude

Ironically, in America where Christianity is the dominant faith, demonic influences are prevalent and are increasing. As you read this book, you'll clearly see how Satan's demons are powerfully affecting the minds and behaviors of the young, old, men, women, Christians (the Church), and unbelievers regardless of their ethnicity and religious backgrounds.

Who is Satan, the devil, and does he truly exist? Satan is Lucifer, he's truly alive, and he's extremely busy spiritually influencing people to ignore God's word. Prior to Lucifer's removal from heaven, he was a powerful and extremely handsome archangel in charge of the heaven choir. <u>He wanted to be God and rebelled along with his recruited angels to overthrow the Creator.</u> The archangel, Michael and his angels, fought against Lucifer and his angels, defeated them, and threw them out of heaven into the earthly realm where Satan has set up his throne to rule above the stars. Satan remains to this day going back and forth to heaven approaching God to point out man's failings that he influenced to happen. The fallen angels are now demons, and their primary purpose is to help Lucifer (Satan) destroy mankind spiritually and physically.

<u>Revelation 12</u>: **"(7)And, there was war in heaven: Michael and his angels fought against the dragon: and the dragon fought and his angels,**

8

The "Falling Away"

[8]And prevailed not; neither was their place found any more in Heaven. [9]And the great dragon was cast out, that old serpent, called the Devil and Satan, which deceiveth the whole world: he was cast out into the earth, and his angels were cast out with him."

Revelation 12: "[12]Therefore, rejoice O heaven and you that dwell therein! Woe to the inhabitants of the earth and of the sea! For the devil is come down unto you, having great wrath, because he knoweth that he hath but a short time."

Isaiah 14: "[12]How art thou <u>fallen</u> from heaven, O Lucifer, son of the morning! How art thou cut down to the ground, which didst weaken the nations! [13]For thou has said in thine heart, I will ascend into Heaven, I will exalt my <u>throne above the stars of God</u>: I will sit also upon the mount of the congregation, in the sides of the north: [14]I will ascend above the heights of the clouds; <u>I will be like the most High.</u> [15]Yet thou shalt be brought down to hell to the sides of the pit."

I Peter 5: "[8]Be sober, be vigilant (alert) because your adversary the devil, as a roaring lion, walketh about seeking whom he may devour."

Job 2: "[1] Again there was a day when the sons of God came to present themselves before the Lord, and Satan came also among them to present

The "Falling Away"

himself before the Lord. (2)And the Lord said unto Satan, from whence comest thou? And Satan answered the Lord, and said, from going to and fro in the earth, and from walking up and down in it."

The above scriptures confirm where Lucifer came from; where he is today; that he has access to the throne of God; he walks the earth; and, he goes back and forth inside the earth to hell. Hell, Satan's final destination, is located in the center of the earth.

Now that we know precisely who Satan is, be assured that he and his demons have been and are busy influencing the human race to turn away from God's ways without having remorse. These influences have brought about the **"Falling Away"** epoch that the world is blindly and currently experiencing.

In **II Thessalonians 2:3,** Apostle Paul warns us that before the **"Coming of the Lord"**, there will be a **"Falling Away"** which is when mankind will turn away from God's laws and live sinful lifestyles without fear or remorse.

Sometime during the climax of this evil period of man's disobedience against God, the **"Son of Perdition"** also known as the **"Antichrist"** and as the **"Son of Satan"** will manifest. He will come in disguise as a brilliant man of peace and will eventually bring worldwide peace to gain favor of the human race.

The "Falling Away"

Currently, the **"New War" with Iraq** that's about to erupt is going to escalate and cause continuous catastrophes to develop throughout the world for many years to come. These times are referred to in the Bible as "The beginning of Sorrows." The stage is being set for the **"Antichrist"** to come and reign as the world leader. What a deceiver this great leader will be. Once in power, he'll convince the majority of the people throughout the world that he is God and will reign in the temple in Jerusalem. Many Jews will believe that he's the Messiah. Several years after being in power, the **"Antichrist"** will demonstrate the true meaning of **EVIL** that the world has never known.

II Thessalonians 2: **"[4]Who opposeth and exalteth himself above all that is called God, or that is worshipped; so that he as God sitteth in the temple of God, showing himself that he is God."**

Since Satan cannot create life to produce a son, I believe there is a possibility that the **"Antichrist"** will be a **cloned** individual possessed by a powerful demon. Consider the fact that **cloning**, creating mankind, falls right into Satan's thought process - impersonating God in creating life. Even though it is not legal to clone human beings, there's a possibility it is secretly happening somewhere. With the existing evil influences prevailing, the temptation would be too great to resist.

11

The "Falling Away"

No one knows how far we are into the climax of the **"Falling Away."** However, with scriptural evidence of what to look for already aggressively prevailing throughout the world, I believe that we're near the **finale**. Therefore, I believe that the **"Antichrist"** is already in the world; and, at this time, he's unaware of who and what his destiny is. He has not, **yet**, been empowered with Satan's demonic spirit.

As the <u>god</u> of this world, Satan is aware that he's running out of time, and his ultimate plan is to take as many people with him to hades/hell as he possibly can. **Hell is where the fire shall never be quenched (Mark 9:43).**

In reiterating that the enormous increase and acceptance of sinful lifestyles lead to eternal destruction, it is unfortunate that the majority of the people in this world are blindly headed in that direction.

The below scripture confirms that the pathway to heaven is narrow, straight, and that there will be few who find it.

<u>Matthew 7</u>: **"(13)Enter ye in at the straight gate: for wide is the gate, and broad is the way that leadeth to destruction, and many there be which go in thereat: (14)Because straight is the gate, and narrow is the way, which leadeth unto life, and few there be that find it."**

The "Falling Away"

What mankind must realize is that **WE ARE SPIRITS THAT HAVE A SOUL AND LIVE IN A PHYSICAL BODY.** Our spirits are serving God, the creator of every living creature **OR** are serving the god of this world, Satan, and don't know it.

Mathew 6: **"[24]No man can serve two masters: for either he will hate the one, and love the other; or else he will hold to the one, and despise the other. Ye cannot serve God and mammon (sell your soul to the devil for riches and worldly gain)."**

Ecclesiastes 1: **"[9]The thing that hath been it is that which shall be; and that which is done is that which shall be done; and there is no new thing under the sun."**

The second above scripture clearly says that demonic influences existing in this world are not new. The demonic influence that has homosexuality rapidly increasing throughout the world existed before in the cities of **Sodom and Gomorrah.** Everyone, except Lot and his family, in those two cities became homosexuals because of Satan's influence; and, God destroyed everyone including the cities with fire because of the abomination. **God is not only a man of love but of war.** He destroyed mankind with a flood sparing only Noah and his family because Satan's influences had consumed the entire human race with evil causing them to reject His laws. God is

13

a jealous God, and He created mankind to worship and serve Him not Satan.

Exodus 15: "(3)The LORD is a man of war: the LORD is his name."

Luke 17: "(26)And as it was in the days of Noah, so shall it be also in the days of the Son of man. They did eat, they drank, they married wives, they were given in marriage, until the day that Noah entered into the ark, and the flood came, and destroyed them all. Likewise also as it was in the days of Lot; they did eat, they drank, they bought, they sold, they planted, they built; But the same day that Lot went out of Sodom it rained fire and brimstone from Heaven, and destroyed them all. Even thus shall it be in the day when the Son of man is revealed."

The second above scripture is saying that people in the world will be performing their daily routines when Christ returns (the rapture takes place) for His church.

Exodus 34: "(14)Thou shalt worship no other god: for the LORD, whose name is Jealous, is a jealous God."

Deuteronomy 6: "(15)For the LORD thy God is a jealous God among you lest the anger of the LORD thy God be kindled against thee, and destroy thee from off the face of the earth."

The "Falling Away"

Ecclesiastes 12: "⁽¹³⁾Let us hear the conclusion of the whole matter. <u>Fear God and keep his commandments: for this is the whole duty of man.</u> ⁽¹⁴⁾For God shall bring every work into judgment with every secret thing, whether it be good or whether it be evil."

I'm confident that final destruction of this world, as it exists today, is not so far away. As you read this book, I pray that your spiritual ears and eyes will open to recognize the TRUTH. Should you find yourself identifying with any of the described characteristics, let there be no self-condemnation. This is not the purpose of my writings. Instead, allow the contents of this book motivate you towards taking the necessary redemptive steps in accepting Jesus Christ as your Lord and Savior, who died for all of our sins.

Titus 2: "⁽¹⁴⁾Who gave himself for us, that he might redeem us from all iniquity and purify unto himself a peculiar people, zealous of good works."

Keep in mind that acceptable and unacceptable standards of this world cannot be compared to God's standards.

Isaiah 55: "⁽⁸⁾For my thoughts are not your thoughts, neither are your ways my ways saith the Lord. ⁽⁹⁾For as the heavens are higher than the earth, so are my ways higher than your ways, and my thoughts than your thoughts."

The "Falling Away"

Now, let's take a look at what God says we will see during the "Falling Away."

The "Falling Away"

Chapter One
What is the "Falling Away?"

Ever since I was a child, I heard rumors that the end of the world was coming, and that we're living in the last days. Even when Jesus Christ was on earth, people were concerned about the end of time being near. God, however, would not have us ignorant of this important occurrence. His word clearly confirms what events will happen prior to the end so that Christians would know. Since Satan has the majority of the human race spiritually blind, deaf, and disconnected from God, they're unaware that the world is currently headed towards destruction and why.

Apostle Paul, inspired by the Holy Spirit, wrote most of the New Testament in the Bible. He warned the Thessalonians, more than 2,000 years ago, not to fear about the end of the world coming. He said there must **first** be a **"Falling Away"** **AND** that the **"Son of Satan"** must manifest before Christ returns for His **"Church"**, the true Christians. This event is known as the **"Rapture"**. The **"Rapture"** will occur following two major events:

(1) The "Falling Away" is when demonic spiritual influences turn the majority of mankind against God's ways.

(2) Manifestation of the "Son of Satan" also known as the "Antichrist."

It's important to know that our calculation of time is not the same as God's. **One thousand years of our time is one (1) day to God**. Theologians say that Christ has been gone for 2,000 years. No one knows exactly how long Christ has been gone. I believe that Christ's departure time frame is closer to that of 3,000 years (3 days to God). Why? By comparing Biblical description of the **"Falling Away"** to what's happening in the world today. The number (3) is a significant number to God. It represents the Trinity (i.e., Father, Son and Holy Ghost). Jesus rose from the grave on the third (3rd) day, and I believe that he's coming for His church **(the Rapture)** on the **third (3rd)** day which will be when three thousand years our time have elapsed since He returned to Heaven.

Scriptural Confirmation that one (1) day to God is one thousand years of earth time:

II Peter 3: "$^{(8)}$But, beloved, be not ignorant of this one thing, that one day is with the Lord as a thousand years, and a thousand years as one day."

Scriptural Confirmation that the "Rapture" will come after the "Falling Away" and the "Son of Satan" is revealed:

The "Falling Away"

II Thessalonians 2: [1]Now we beseech you, brethren, by the coming of our Lord Jesus Christ, and by our gathering together unto him (Rapture). [2]That ye be not soon shaken in mind, or be troubled, neither by spirit, nor by word, not by letter as from us, as that the day of Christ is at Hand. [3]Let no man deceive you by any means: FOR THAT DAY SHALL NOT COME, EXCEPT THERE COME A "Falling Away" first, and that man of sin be revealed, the "Son of Perdition"; [4]who opposeth and exalteth himself above all that is called God, or that is worshipped; so that he as God sitteth in the temple of God, showing himself that he is God."

So, what is the **"Falling Away?"**

The following scriptures clearly depict what the **"Falling Away"** is:

I Timothy 4: "[1]Now, the Spirit (Holy Spirit) speaketh expressly that in the latter times (today) some shall depart from the Faith (God's word), giving heed to seducing spirits (consulting psychics, witchcraft, etc.) and doctrines of devils (any religion that deters from God's word) [2] speaking lies in hypocrisy (double standard – say one thing and do another) having their conscience seared with a hot iron (no conscience or remorse – evil doing is acceptable); [3]Forbidding to marry (living together as husband and wife without being married), and commanding to abstain from meats, which God hath created to be received with thanksgiving of them which believe and know the truth (vegetarians have become a popular trend) [4]For every creature of God is good, and nothing to be refused if it be received with thanksgiving (to bless it). [5] For it is sanctified by the word of God and prayer."

II Timothy 3: "[1]This know also, that in the last days (present days) perilous times shall come. [2]For men shall be lovers of their own selves, covetous (jealous, greedy), boasters (to brag and esteem himself more than another), blasphemers (to speak against God's word), disobedient to parents, unthankful, unholy, [3]Without natural affection (lovers of same sex), trucebreakers (when you don't keep promises), false accusers (liars), incontinent (no control over appetite, especially sexual passion), fierce (violent), despisers of those that are good, [4]traitors, heady, high-minded, lovers of pleasures more than lovers of God: [5]Having a form of godliness but denying the power thereof (pretenders); from such turn away. [6]For of this sort are they which creep into houses, and lead captive silly women laden with sins, led away with divers (different kinds) of lusts (sins), [7]ever learning, and never able to come to the knowledge of the truth".

Proverbs 1: "[7]The fear of the Lord is the beginning of knowledge: but fools despise wisdom and instruction."

Now that you've read what God says about the "Falling Away." let's look at the characteristics that will increase among mankind during this prophetic time that are described in the following chapters.

The "Falling Away"

Chapter Two
Departure from the Faith

Today's Christianity is comprised of three groups: 1) The True Christian, 2) The Carnal-Minded Christian, and 3) The Carnal-Spiritual Minded Christian.

The majority of Christians today are unaware of the nature of evil spirits (demons). They choose to ignore this portion of the Bible because of fearing things that are beyond their carnal understanding. There is a need for more teaching about evil spirits and their three main identifying marks which are: **a) to enslave, b) defile and c) torment.** Evil influences have caused the majority of Christian denominations to **fall away** from the truth of God just like the self-righteous Pharisees. Today's Christians are worshiping God in a traditional manner rather than in **Spirit and Truth.** Christian denominations are becoming "Cults" without realizing it because of Satan's influences.

Matthew 5: "**(20)For I say unto you that except your righteousness exceed the righteousness of the scribes and Pharisees, ye shall in no case enter into the kingdom of Heaven.**"

John 4: "**(23)But the hour cometh and now is, when the true worshippers shall worship the Father in the spirit (anointing of the Holy**

Spirit) and truth (knowledge and obedience to the written word of God)."

1. **The True Christian:**
   True Christians are sinners who have accepted Jesus Christ as the Son of God. Metaphorically, God refers to Christians as "The body of Christ" because He uses us to do His deeds. Christians practice on a daily basis living in obedience to God's laws and are influenced by **OR** are filled with the "Holy Spirit" who leads and guides them into all truths. Even though Christians will fall into disobedience from time to time, they don't practice it. Christians, after committing a sin(s), experience discomfort and excruciating spiritual pain that is caused by God's chastisement. This spiritual punishment is more significant than the punishment of our parent(s) as children. As believers become closer to God by studying His word, disobedience becomes less. Becoming sinless is impossible because everyone including Christians falls short of perfection. The flesh will not allow one to become sinless because sin dwells in the flesh.

   The below scriptures describes the lusts of the flesh.

Galatians 5: "[16]This I say then, walk in the Spirit and ye shall not fulfill the lust of the flesh. [17]For the flesh lusteth against the spirit, and the spirit against the flesh: and these are contrary the one to the other: so that ye cannot do the things that ye would [18]But if ye be led by the Spirit, ye are not under the law. [19]Now the works of the flesh are manifest, which are Adultery, fornication, uncleanness, lasciviousness, [20]Idolatry, witchcraft, hatred, variance, emulations, wrath, strife, seditions, heresies, [21]Envy, murder, drunkenness, revellings (an uproaring party), and such like: of the which I tell you before, as I have also told you in time past, that they which do such things shall not inherit the kingdom of God."**

Galatians 5: "[24]And, they that are Christ's have crucified the flesh with the affections and lusts."**

True Christians fear disobeying God, are knowledgeable of His word, and have the influence of **OR** are filled with the "Holy Spirit" who empowers them to resist sinful desires when tempted. The Spirit of God dwells inside of true Christians to help them to do right when the flesh says to do wrong. Satan is always present to inveigle us, but he has no power over a strong believer and doer of the word. God does test us, but he doesn't tempt us.

James 1: "**(13)Let no man say when he is tempted, I am tempted of God: for God cannot be tempted with evil, neither tempteth he any man.**"

James 1: "**(14)But every man is tempted, when he is drawn away of his own lust, and enticed.**"

Many sinful spiritual influences (temptations) are derived from enticements of people in our lives. This is why God warns us not to be involved with unbelievers on a personal basis.

II Corinthians 6: "**(14)Be ye not unequally yoked with unbelievers. For what fellowship hath righteousness with unrighteousness? And, what communion hath light with darkness?**

It is when we live in obedience to the word that we have power over all of Satan's influences.

Luke 10: "**(19)Behold, I give unto you power to tread on serpents and scorpions, and over**

all the powers of the enemy: and nothing shall by any means hurt you."

II Corinthians 5: "(17) Therefore if any man be in Christ, he is a new creature: old things are passed away; behold all things are become new. (18)And all things are of God, who hath reconciled us to himself by Jesus Christ, <u>and hath given to us the ministry of reconciliation</u>; (19)To witness, that God was in Christ, reconciling the world unto himself, not imputing their trespasses unto them; and hath committed unto us the word of reconciliation."

True Christians are ministers of Christ. They are to be fishermen of men for the Kingdom of God.

2. **Carnal Minded Christians**:
Carnal minded Christians have **departed from the Faith**. These Christians believe that Christ is the **"Son of God"** but lack knowledge of the word and power of the Holy Spirit that enables them to live in obedience. They are spiritually dead and disconnected from God. When one is spiritually dead, he or she has not been reborn by renewing his or her mind to God's ways and are not influenced by **OR** are filled with the Holy Spirit. Demonic influences or demon possession dominates their lifestyles. <u>They</u>

lean on their own understanding as to what is acceptable or unacceptable based on the world's carnal standards.

Romans 8: "[5]For they that are after the flesh do mind the things of the flesh; but they that are after the Spirit the things of the Spirit. [6]For to be carnally minded is death; but to be spiritually minded is life and peace. [7]Because the carnal mind is enmity against God: for it is not subject to the law of God, neither indeed can be."

Matthew 7: "[21]Not everyone that saith unto me, Lord, Lord, shall enter into the kingdom of heaven; but he that doeth the will of my Father which is in Heaven."

Matthew 10: "[32]Whosoever therefore shall confess me before men, him will I confess also before my father which is in Heaven."

John 3: "[15]That whosoever believeth in him should not perish, but have eternal life."

Proverbs 3: "[5]Trust in the Lord with all your heart; and, lean not unto your own understanding; [6]In all your ways acknowledge Him; and, He shall direct thy paths. "[7]Be not wise in thine own eyes: fear the Lord, and depart from evil."

Christianity is a lifestyle based on living in obedience to the laws of God. It is not a religion. It is impossible to please God without faith; and, one cannot have faith in God without having knowledge of the word.

<u>James 2</u>: "[19]Thou believe that there is one God; thou doest well: the devils also believe and tremble."

Carnal minded Christians believe but they don't react to God's law. Some faithfully go to the "House of Worship," participate in various auxiliaries, pay tithes and believe that they're saved while practicing sin on a daily basis with no remorse. Satan has them blinded and deaf to the truth.

<u>James 1</u>: "[21]Wherefore lay apart all filthiness and superfluity (over indulgence) of naughtiness, and receive with meekness the engrafted word, which is able to save your souls. [22]But be ye doers of the word, and not hearers only, deceiving your own selves."

The "Falling Away"

2. **The Carnal Spiritual Christians:**
   Carnal spiritual minded Christians are hypocritical. They're the same as the carnal minded Christians with the exception that they believe in the spiritual gifts of the **"Holy Spirit"**. They have double standards and pretend that they're **"holy"**. These Christians prophecy, lay hands on the sick, speak in tongues, sometimes charge money for the use of their gifts and secretly live sinful lives. Satan is using them as vessels. Their exemplified powers are that of Satan and not of God. They're not true Christians and are blinded by demonic spiritual influence. Foolishly, they believe that they're of God because of their spiritual abilities. **They are of the god of this world, Satan,** who is extremely deceitful and knows how to convince the minds of mankind that they're righteous, when they're actually his servants.

Matthew 7: **"(21)Not everyone that saith unto me, Lord, Lord, shall enter into the kingdom of heaven; but he that doeth the will of my father which is in heaven. (22) Many will say to me in that day, Lord, Lord, have we not prophesied in thy name? And in thy name have cast out devils? And in thy name done many wonderful works? (23)And then will I profess unto them, I never knew you: depart from me, ye that work iniquity.**

The "Falling Away"

What about those who don't believe in the existence of God?

<u>Atheist or Non-Believing Individuals</u>:
These people are carnal minded and spiritually disconnected from God. Not all carnal minded people practice evil deeds. Many atheists are loving and wonderful people who live more righteous lifestyles than those confessing to know God. Unfortunately, because of their disbelief and none acceptance of Jesus Christ as the "Son of God," they're spiritually disconnected and are considered lost to God. They will not have eternal life in heaven regardless of their goodness.

<u>John 14</u>: "[6]Jesus saith unto him, I am the way, the truth, and the life: no man cometh unto the Father, but by me."

<u>Today's Christian Denominations Lack the "Holy Spirit" Influences:</u>

The lack of the **"Holy Spirit"** influences **AND** the evidence of demonic influences exists in far too many established Christian denominations today. These establishments are becoming Christian **"cults"** because they've fallen away from the truth. Their worshiping is that of tradition not **Spirit** and **Truth**. They mention the **"Holy Spirit,"** but **don't believe** in the gifts of the **Spirit**, (e.g., prophesying, laying of hands, speaking in tongues). These gifts are evidence of the presence of God. One cannot interpret God's word accurately without the influence of **OR** being filled with the **"Holy Spirit"**. Therefore, congregations are suffering from lack of knowledge of how to proclaim and use God's word as a weapon **(Hebrew 4:12)** to combat the enemy **AND** as a tool to bring the promises of God from the spiritual realm into the physical realm. God has promised His children abundant life in all aspects. Far too many Christians are suffering because of their lack of knowledge and faith.

Like the disciple, doubting Thomas, who didn't believe that Christ had risen from the dead until he saw him with his eyes and touched him with his hands, so are most Christians. They don't live by faith in the promises of God. Didn't Christ say that greater works shall we do than He? He was powerful after the **"Holy Spirit"** came upon him. He gave sight to the blind, raised the dead, turned water into wine, and fed thousands by miraculously increasing a small amount of bread and fish. **Do we see greater works being performed in the "Houses of Worship" by the Pastors or body of Christ today?** The answer is NO. Why? BECAUSE they lack knowledge of the word, faith in the word, and are not filled with the Holy Spirit. The majority of believers in today's Church (body of Christ) are powerless when it

The "Falling Away"

comes to performing spiritual gifts. There is a great deal of biblical motivational speaking about prosperity taking place in the "House of Wishop" these days vs. obedience. No wonder immorality is increasing and becoming the normal lifestyle for mankind.

John 14: **"(12)Verily, verily, I say unto you, he that believeth on me, the works that I do shall he do also; and greater works than these shall he do; because I go unto my Father."**

Mark 16: **"(17)And these signs shall follow them that believe; in my name shall they cast out devils; they shall speak with new tongues; (18) They shall take up serpents; and if they drink any deadly thing, it shall not hurt them; they shall lay hands on the sick, and they shall recover."**

The power that is referenced in the above scriptures **does exist** today among believers who are hearers and doers of God's law. Congregations consist of believers who are mentally, physically and spiritually sick. God's blessing of laying hands to receive healing doesn't exist in most "Houses of Worship" especially those that are none Pentecost. Some Pastor(s) obviously don't believe that God's healing is available today. These Pastors are not called by God to be over His church.

The "Falling Away"

How can God's people be edified without the manifestation of the spiritual gifts? Doesn't God say in His word that He's present when two or more are gathered in His name? God is a Spirit, and when He's present, be assured there will be spiritual gifts at work. When one is called by God to lead or preside over His people, that leader will be empowered with the anointing of **"Holy Spirit."** God has not changed. He uses ordinary people and makes them extraordinary.

Luke 9: "[1]**And he called the twelve (disciples) together and gave them** <u>**power and authority**</u> **over all demons and to cure diseases.**"

Acts 1: "[8]**But you shall receive** <u>**power**</u> **when the Holy Spirit has come upon you; and you shall be my witnesses in Jerusalem and in all Judea and Samaria and** <u>**to the end of the earth.**</u>"

John 1: "[12]**But to all who received him, who believed in his name, he gave power to become children of God;**"

Hebrew 13: "[8]**Jesus Christ is the same yesterday, today, and forever.**"

God warns us to discern and know who is of Him. It is one's own responsibility to be aware of the truth. I'm not judging. I'm writing about what I've discerned and observed while visiting different

"Houses of Worship" and talking to various Christians.

I Corinthians 2: "[14]The unspiritual (sinner) man does not receive the gifts of the spirit of God, for they are folly to him, and he is not able to understand them because they are <u>spiritually discerned</u>."

II Timothy 2: "[15]Study to show thyself approved unto God, a workman that needeth not to be ashamed, rightly dividing the word of truth."

There are innumerable "cult religions" in existence today whose teachings are similar to that of Christianity; yet, in an extremely subtle way they differ. Some of these religious cults claim God as their Savior and denies that Jesus Christ is the Son of God. Others have altered God's word to accommodate their beliefs, and some only believe in the Old Testament. One of the largest religions in the world, teaches their followers to pray to the mother of Jesus, to disciples, and repent to their Priests. Scripture clearly says that we must pray to the Heavenly Father **through Jesus Christ only. <u>After all, Jesus is the one who redeemed us through the shedding of his blood. He paid the price for our sins – not man</u>**. Prior to Jesus coming to earth, God's people could only pray to the priests for forgiveness, and the priests would pray to God on their behalf. Since Jesus Christ, our creator, came and redeemed us through the shedding of his blood, we are under a new covenant that requires mankind to **pray and repent to Jesus only and not man**.

I Timothy 2: "**[5]For there is one God, and one mediator between God and men, the man Christ Jesus.**"

The crucifixion of Christ was not secretly done but publicly. Yet, Satan's influences have many believing that Jesus Christ was only a teacher, not the Son of God, and that no crucifixion took place. This lie is believed by many "Cult" religions that exist today.

Galatians 3: "**[1]O foolish Galatians! Who has bewitched you, before whose eyes Jesus Christ was publicly portrayed as crucified?**"

Ephesians 1: "**[7]In him (Jesus Christ) we have redemption through his blood, the forgiveness of our trespasses, according to the riches of his grace.**"

Those who don't know God's word can easily be persuaded to accept "cults," because they're deceitful and convincing. Spiritual demonic influences have many people thinking that they're on the straight and narrow path, when they're on the road to eternal destruction. It is necessary to study God's word in order to determine the truth. **Knowledge of God's word guards against accepting false doctrines**.

John 14: "**(6)Jesus said to him, "I am the way, and the truth, and the life; no one comes to the Father, but by me."**

The above scripture confirms that any religion that denies Jesus Christ as the "Son of God" and prays to any other than to the Heavenly Father through Jesus Christ is a cult.

Colossians 2: "**(8)Beware lest any man spoil you through philosophy and vain deceit, after the tradition of men, after the rudiments (fundamentals) of the world, and not after Christ."**

II Peter 2: "**(1)But there were false prophets also among the people, even as there shall be false teachers among you, who privily (secretly) shall bring in damnable heresies (dissent) even denying the Lord that bought them (purchased with the shedding of his blood), and bring upon themselves swift destruction. (2)And many shall follow their pernicious (harmful) ways; by reason of whom the way of truth shall be evil spoken of." (CULTS)**

The "Falling Away"

Globally, terrorists are increasing in number and are becoming more dangerous. They're deceitfully being influenced by Satan to believe they're killing for their God. There is some truth to their belief because Satan is the god of this world; and, they're killing for him. The terrorist's attack on September 11, 2001 in New York had nothing to do with the Muslim religion that advocates peace.

Christians must realize that there are evil forces fighting against mankind every day. God did not leave us defenseless against these forces.

Ephesians 6: **"[11]Put on the whole amour of God that ye may be able to stand against the wiles of the devil, [12]For we wrestle not against flesh and blood but against principalities, against powers, against the rulers of the darkness of this world, against spiritual wickedness in high places. [13]Wherefore take unto you the whole amour of God that ye may be able to withstand in the evil day and having done all, to stand. [14]Stand therefore, having your loins girt about with the truth (knowledge of the word), and having on the breastplate of righteousness (Faith); [15]And your feet shod with the preparation of the gospel of peace. [16]Above all, taking the shield of faith, wherewith ye shall be able to quench all the fiery darts of the wicked."**

The "Falling Away"

The Word is a Weapon:

Hebrew 4: "**[12]For the word of God is quick, and powerful, and sharper than any two edged sword, piercing even to the dividing asunder of soul and spirit, and of the joints and marrow, <u>and is a discerner of the thoughts and intents of the heart.</u>**"

The above scriptures clearly say that our enemies are spirits of darkness, and we must fight them spiritually. This is why God says to worship Him in **Spirit and Truth**. We become spiritual through: **1)** knowledge of the "God's word" which is spirit because the "word" is God and **2)** by being filled with the "Holy Spirit" who gives us powers over satanic attacks.

John 1: "**[1]In the beginning was the word, and the word was with God, and <u>the word was God.</u>**"

The word is powerful isn't it? It is powerful because it is God. God's power is always present to fulfill what He has spoken and promised in scriptures.

Isaiah 55: "**[11]So shall my word be that goeth forth out of my mouth: it shall not return unto me void, but it shall accomplish**

that which I please, and it shall prosper in the thing whereto I sent it."

Unfortunately, many Christians who regularly go to the "House of Worship" lack knowledge of the word. Therefore, their lives lack the benefits of abundant living materially, physically and spiritually.

- Many Pastors do not teach the principles of walking by faith. Far too many Christians lack faith and vision in God's promises because they don't know the word. God has provided abundant living for His people. He healed us when he died on the cross; yet, most Christians are living by sight rather than by faith because they confess having sickness instead of being healed. For example: In **Isaiah 53:** **"[5]God says that "he was wounded for our transgressions, he was bruised for our iniquities: the chastisement of our peace was upon him; and with his stripes (beatings) we are healed."**

This scripture says that we are healed. A believer must take God at His word through faith. When you confess that you're healed by believing what God says in His word and do not confess the physical sickness that you see and feel in the body, this is what makes the sickness leave.

The "Falling Away"

Remember, God's word is a weapon against the enemy. Satan manufactures all diseases. God may allow sickness to come, but Satan is the one to bring them.

Our blessings are in the spiritual realm. By thanking God for those things that you've asked Him for as though you've already received them, this is FAITH. Your faith will bring all blessings you desire and proclaim into your life.

Knowledge is Power. God's people **lack power** because they lack both knowledge of the word and faith in the promises.

Romans 10: "[(17)]So then faith cometh by hearing, and hearing by the word of God."

Matthew 21: "[(21)]Jesus answered and said unto them, Verily I say unto you if ye have faith, and doubt not, ye shall not only do this which is done to the fig tree (Jesus cursed the fig tree and it dried up – POWER), but also if ye shall say unto this mountain (problem or obstacle), be thou removed, and be thou cast into the sea (NONE EXISTENCE), it shall be done.
[(22)]And all things, whatsoever ye shall ask in prayer, believing, ye shall receive."**

- Pastors don't reprove the congregation of their sins – they ignore them. Many Pastors don't reprove their congregation because they are guilty of committing some of the same sins: adultery, greed, fornication, homosexuality, etc. Some Pastors may not be guilty of visible sinful conduct but guilty of inward lusts.

Financial greed is prevalent among Pastors. Many won't reprove members of their congregations because they fear losing the membership and the large amount of money given. This is evident, particularly, with the Pastors whose congregations consist of famous entertainers (e.g., singers who sing sinful lyrics, wear seductive clothing and dance with sexual overtones on stage, and actors who perform adulterous, murdering, pornography, and other perverted and abominable roles). Entertainers such as these are unknowingly committing sin against God for fame and wealth. In other words, they have sold their souls to the devil for fame and wealth. Pastors have a responsibility to let their congregation know when they're practicing disobedience to God's word. Entertainers have a powerful affect on influencing the behavior of many.

When a Pastor is truly called by God, he will not compromise God's word and will speak against the sins dominating the lives of his congregation by teaching the appropriate scriptures. **A Pastor's lack of reprimand is silent acceptance,** and that is dangerously misleading to those who think they're right with God when they're actually on the path way to hell.

A Pastor who is not operating under the anointing and instruction of God is going to be held accountable for misleading the body of Christ from the truth. Being summons by God to Pastor a congregation is the highest calling. It is extremely detrimental to the body of Christ when a Pastor is not called by God.

II Timothy 4: **"(2)Preach the word; be instant in season, out of season; reprove, rebuke, exhort with all long suffering and doctrine."**

Throughout the world, there is an increased and strong demonic influence of **incontinence.** In other words, there is no control over sexual appetite. Sexual perversions are becoming popular and are promoted big time in the movies, music and on the internet. It is amazing to see entertainers who write or sing evil lyrics and those who have performed abominable roles in movies, accepting awards and thanking God for their success. This is a perfect example of walking in darkness. God, the creator, has absolutely nothing to do with their success. Demonic blindness and deceit are present in these instances. Remember one cannot serve God and mammon. You can't commit adultery in the name of acting or write a song about killing and fornicating and think God is in agreement with what you're doing. This does not apply to all entertainers. Some singers carefully choose their lyrics. There's a big difference in singing about love versus sexual indulgence. Sex was created to be private and sacred between the husband and wife. The entertainment arena is inundated with demonic influences because Satan loves entertainment. In heaven, he was in charge of the choir. To this day, Satan continues to be intrigued with music and inspires the writing of many evil lyrics and movies that are popular.

Satan is the god of this world, and he blesses those of disobedience just as God, the creator, blesses His children of obedience. Satan can and will take a person to the peak of success in this world just to have his soul in the end. Even if one lives to become 90 years old, that time is short compared to the never-ending lifetime that follows this earthly existence. Therefore, to sell one's soul to Satan for fame and wealth is a foolish decision. Eternal life is forever and ever, and there's no end. The

The "Falling Away"

decisions we make in this world will
determine our everlasting final destination.

I Timothy 6: "**(10)For the <u>love of money is
the root of all evil</u>: which while some
coveted after, they have erred from the
faith, and pierced themselves through with
many sorrows.**"

Many people misquote the above scripture.
There is nothing evil about money. It is what
some do to get money that is evil. Some
people love money to the extent of doing
anything evil and imaginable to get it.

- Pastor(s) are marrying same sex partners
  (homosexuals) as well as marrying men and
  women who have been divorced numerous
  times while previous spouses are still living.

God ordains marriages between men and
women for His children who are Christians.
Therefore, in this world, there appears to be
two types of marriages: **1) Christian
marriage - where God's laws are honored**,
and **2) Worldly marriage – is conditional
and rules do not apply to God's laws.**

Matthew 19: "**(9)And, I say unto you,
whosoever shall put away (divorce) his wife,
<u>EXCEPT</u> it be for fornication and shall**

The "Falling Away"

marry another, committeth adultery: and who marrieth her which is put away doth commit adultery."

Even though we're living in the 21st Century, God's word is unchanging. There was a time not so long ago when the law of the land would not allow a husband and wife to get a divorce except for the reasons stipulated in God's word. Today, one can get a divorce simply because he or she desires to do so, and homosexuals can legally marry. This is another example of the **"Falling Away"** from the word. Pastors and judges that are granting divorces and marriages by disobeying guidelines set by God will one day be required to give an account for their disobedience. The laws of this world are rapidly changing to oppose God's laws because of the carnal minded law makers. Christians are to obey only the laws that are not in conflict with God's word. After all, according to scripture, we are not of this world and are not to transform to the ways of it. We're just traveling through.

Romans 12: "$^{(22)}$**And be not conformed to this world: but be ye transformed by the renewing of your mind, that ye may prove what is that good, and acceptable, and perfect, will of God."**

The "Falling Away"

Revelation 4: "**(14)I know thy works, that thou art neither cold nor hot: I would thou wert cold or hot. (16)So then because thou art lukewarm, and neither cold nor hot, I will spit thee out of my mouth.**"

The majority of today's Christians are lukewarm, and God has no use for a lukewarm believer. Metaphorically, an atheist is considered cold, a disobedient believer is lukewarm, and a true believer is HOT.

I personally believe that a true WARNING of whether something is acceptable to God is to observe the world's acceptance of it. Since Satan is the god of this world, whatever is popular – you can be assured it is not acceptable with God.

The "Falling Away"

Increasing ABOMINATIONS

Deuteronomy 18: "[18]There shall not be found among you anyone that maketh his son or his daughter to pass through the fire (hell), or that useth divination, or an observer of times, or an enchanter, or a witch, [11]or a charmer, or a consulter with familiar spirits (demons), or a wizard, or necromancer (communicator with the dead). [12]For all that do these things are an <u>abomination</u> unto the Lord: and because of these abominations, the Lord thy God doth drive them out from before thee."

Throughout the world, it is becoming very popular among people to consult with card readers, necromancers (communicating with the dead), palm readers, psychics, witches and warlocks. They are also known as **"ministers of darkness."** Their services consist of: predicting the future, putting curses on others, love spells, etc. Those who do not resort to these practices will be shocked at the damage that can occur to one's life through these evil channels of darkness.

Many marriages exist because of witchcraft practices. These marriages are bound by Satan to bring misery or even death. The man or woman victimized by witchcraft feels that something isn't right; yet, he or she is not aware that the nagging mental distress of unhappiness is due to a curse.

Some carnal minded Christians are just as guilty as unbelievers by seeking ungodly counseling from "**ministers of darkness**." By doing so is acknowledging Satan as your God even if you lack knowledge of this fact.

God uses Christian people with the gift of prophecy to speak to His children, and Satan does the same through His "**ministers of darkness**." They are connected to "familiar spirits" who are also referred to as demons. Demons have been present since the beginning of time and are familiar with past and current incidents that occur in our life. Their spiritual influences have a profound impact on negativities affecting mankind.

There are five ways one can know the future: **a)** revelation by the Holy Spirit, **b)** visions from God, **c)** dreams from God, **d)** prophecies from Christians filled with the Holy Spirit, and **e)** communicating with "**ministers of da**rkness" who communicates with "familiar spirits (demons)." In this case, usually lies are told with the truth.
Demonic influences can also direct evil people into one's life who will appear as perfect human

beings. This is why God tells us to discern the spirits and know who is of Him.

II Corinthians 11: "**(14)And marvel not; for Satan himself is transformed into an angel of light (appearing to be good). (15)Therefore, it is no great thing if <u>his ministers</u> (psychics, witches, warlocks, and false prophets) also be transformed as the ministers of righteousness; whose end shall be according to their works.**"

Spiritual influences of darkness have the world so blinded, that the majority of people don't believe that God or Satan exist; therefore, there's no fear of either. Their disbeliefs will lead to eternal destruction. God warns us in His word that He not only loves us, but that He's quite capable of destroying us because of our disobedience.

Matthew 10: "**(28)Fear not them which kill the body, but are not able to kill the soul: but rather fear Him which is able to destroy both soul and body in hell.**"

Curiosity about the future is not sinful. God created this characteristic within each of us. He sent the **"Holy Spirit"** to lead and guide Christians the right way and to show them future events.

The "Falling Away"

John 16: "**(13)** Howbeit when <u>he</u>, the Spirit of Truth (Holy Spirit), is come, he will guide you into all truth: for he shall not speak of himself; but whatsoever he shall hear (from the heavenly father) that shall he speak; <u>and he will show you things to come.</u> (14)He shall glorify me (God); for he shall receive of mine, and shall show it unto you."

The presence of the "Holy Spirit" dwelling in Christians helps them to do right when the flesh entices them to do wrong. This is the primary reason why God sent Him. Also, the "Holy Spirit" empowers Christians with the power of God, and enables them to interpret God's word with spiritual comprehension. As Christians become spiritually connected to God, they begin to hear His voice speak to them and are able to see the future through dreams and visions that are given by God.

Acts 2: "**(17)**And, in the last days it shall be, God declares that I will pour out my Spirit upon all flesh, and your sons and your daughters shall prophesy, and your young men shall see visions, and your old men shall dream dreams."

The influence of psychic or witchcraft has existed since the beginning of mankind because of Satan. <u>Cursing</u> in the Bible is not only speaking evil of someone, but evil coming upon someone. If a person is under a curse, according to the Bible, evil has come upon that person in some way (e.g., sickness, tragedy, or bad circumstances).

Note: This does not mean that every difficult experience you have is a demonic curse. Sometimes God allows us to experience difficult times that are biblically described as trials or tribulations to increase our faith. These difficulties are blessings in disguise. They allow us to experience His overcoming power, grow stronger, and identify ourselves with Him through sufferings.

Tattooing

When I was a teenager in the late 60's, tattooing was only seen on soldiers returning from overseas. In America today, tattooing and multiple earring piercing on the body is extreme among females and males. What I'm about to say may be shocking to most readers. These trends originate from **witchcraft** roots. Tattoos open spiritual doors for dangerous demonic spirits. The Bible warns us against tattoos in the below scripture.

Leviticus 19: "**(28)Ye shall not make any cuttings in your flesh for the dead, nor print or tattoo any marks upon you: I am the Lord.**"

The "Falling Away"

Deuteronomy 14: "[1]Ye are the sons of the Lord your God; you shall not cut yourselves, nor make any baldness on your foreheads for the dead."

When the above scriptures speak about the dead, this is in relation to a witchcraft ritual that was done in ancient days and today within some pagan cultures to mourn their dead. Tattooing, cutting one's body and shaving one's head in defiance have their origin in witchcraft practices.

Today, tattoo businesses are everywhere because the United States has opened its doors to heathen practices and false religions. Tattooing has opened doors to death by transmitting **AIDS** and **Hepatitis**.

Question: I have tattoos. I didn't know when I got them that I was disobeying God. Will He accept me as a Christian?

Answer: YES. The Lord loves us and will not condemn anyone because of mistakes. However, it is necessary to pray and ask God for forgiveness and pray against any evil influences that may be occurring because of the tattoo.

God is a forgiving God. He knows that all of us are guilty of making mistakes while walking in darkness. When we repent to God, He forgives and forgets our sins.

Isaiah 43: **"(25)I am He who blots out your transgressions for my own sake, and I will not remember your sins."**

The increased popularity of tattooing in today's society doesn't make it right or acceptable with God. Anyone who has been subjected to a witchcraft curse of any kind can be delivered by God's power. There is no need to fear the powers of darkness when you strongly believe in the power of the Light, Jesus Christ.

God's word is not obsolete. The bible consists of scriptures that pertain to every aspect of our lives. Many say that the word is obsolete, and that it doesn't apply to modern times. God and His word are the same. How is God, the creator of time and every living creature, OBSOLETE? Does man know more than the CREATOR?

John 1: **"(1) In the beginning was the word and the word was with God, and the word was God. (2)The same was in the beginning with God. (3)All things were made by him and without him was not anything made that was made. (4)In him was life, and the life was the light of men. (5)And, the light shineth in darkness, and the darkness comprehended it not. (10) He was in**

the world, and <u>the world was made by him</u>, and the world knew him not. ⁽¹¹⁾ He came unto His own and His own received Him not."

<u>Hebrew 13</u>: "⁽⁸⁾Jesus Christ is the same yesterday, today, and forever."

JESUS CHRIST IS THE WORD
HE IS GOD AND THE CREATOR

Keep in mind that the Creator made Satan who is the **god** of this world. Satan uses psychics to prophecy the future; **AND** God uses his children, Christians, who are filled with the Holy Spirit to prophecy the future.

Satan, desiring to be like God, attempts to mimic Him. Remember the story when Moses went before King Pharaoh and threw down his rod that became a large snake? What happened? King Pharaoh's sorcerers, "**ministers of darkness**," threw down their rods and they became **several snakes**? This was clearly a demonstration of Satan's powers. God's **one snake** consumed all the demonic snakes. Satan's power cannot defeat the power of God.

Therefore, if you are consulting with psychics or any demonic counseling, know that this is an abomination to the creator, God.

The "Falling Away"

Chapter Four
Speaking Lies in Two-Facedness
(Pretense and Double Standard)

<u>Proverbs 6</u>: <u>[16]These six things doth the Lord hate: yes, seven are an abomination unto him: [17]A proud look, a lying tongue, and hands that shed innocent blood, [18]A heart that deviseth wicked imaginations, feet that be swift in running to mischief, [19]A false witness that speaketh lies, and he that soweth discord among brethren (troublemaker)</u>."

<u>Colossians 3</u>: "[9]Do not lie to one another, seeing that you have put off the old nature with its practices [10]and have put on the new nature, which is being renewed in knowledge after the image of its creator."

Since unbelievers are not familiar with the word and don't have the influence of **OR** are filled with the **"Holy Spirit,"** they're more prone to fall into one of the seven abominable categories than those who have knowledge of the word.

a) **Proud Look:** Demonic influence of arrogance can easily become a part of one's character when one gets much attention and respect from others because of physical beauty, wealth, etc. God warns us in His word that we are not to esteem ourselves or other individuals as being more than another. People, in general, tend to respect individuals with wealth and ignore the poor. God warns us in His word to be careful how we treat others because there is always the possibility of interacting with an angel who may appear as an ordinary person. Wouldn't it be terrible to have mistreated a poorly dressed individual not knowing he or she was an angel from God in the flesh?

Hebrews 13: **"[2]Be not forgetful to entertain strangers: for thereby some have entertained angels unawares."**

Roman 12: **"[3]For I say, through the grace given unto me, to every man that is among you, not to think of himself more highly than he ought to think; but to think soberly, according as God hath dealt to every man the measure of faith.**

1 John 2: **"[16]For all that is in the world, the lust of the flesh and the lust of the eyes and the pride of life, is not of the Father but is of the world."**

Ezekiel 7: **"[24]I will bring the worst of the nations to take possession of their houses; I will put an end to their proud might, and their holy places shall be profaned."**

Ezekiel 28: "(5)By your great wisdom in trade you have increased your wealth, and your heart has become proud in your wealth."

Ezekiel 28: "(17)Your heart was proud because of your beauty; you corrupted your wisdom for the sake of your splendor. I cast you to the ground; I exposed you before kings, to feast their eyes on you.

A **"Proud Look"** is the attitude that Satan had when he was an archangel in heaven. His physical beauty and musical talent, in heaven, is why he became blindly overconfident in thinking and attempting to defeat God. Arrogance blinded Satan from the truth that God could not be defeated.

b) **Lying Tongue:** Satan is the father of lies, and God is the father of truth. God created words to contain power. He created the world by speaking it into existence. Once words are released from the mouth, they go forth and produce action that consequently returns to you, the sender. One must be careful with the usage of spoken words. The tongue is the smallest member of the body; yet it is the most powerful. Life and death is in the power of the tongue.

The "Falling Away"

James 3: "[5]Even so, the tongue is a little member, and boasteth great things. Behold how great a matter a little fire kindleth. [6] And the tongue is a fire, a world of iniquity: so is the tongue among our members that it defileth the whole body, and setteth on fire the course of nature; and it is set on fire of hell."

The words we speak are filled with lies or truths. Demonic influences of lying and pretentiousness (double standard) are prevalent among mankind today. Lying exists in advertisements, businesses, families, "Houses of Worship", marriages, politics, schools, etc. Mainstream society is not content with their lives. Bogus portrayal of their true identity is ever-present to impress others. Living a lie inevitably confines one to daily torment. Metaphorically, it is like falling into a deep ditch that you daily struggle to climb out of but can't. Much effort is required to live a lie.

God says that we are precious in His sight and for us to be content in whatever state that we're in. Why worry about what man thinks. God is the one to please. Our first priorities should be to impress and please God – not man. By pleasing God, He abundantly and openly rewards us with the blessings we desire.

58

The "Falling Away"

Hebrews 13: "[5]Let your conversation be without covetousness (greed) content with such things as ye have: for he hath said, I will never leave thee, nor forsake thee."

Revelation 21: "[8]The fearful, unbelieving, abominable, murderers, whoremongers, sorcerers, idolaters, and all liars shall have their part in the lack which burneth with fire and brimstone: which is the second death."

Many years ago, a verbal agreement and hand shake was a binding contract. People honored their spoken words. No one wanted to be known as a liar. Today, there is much skepticism in believing what we hear or read because lying is so common. It's amazing how pathological liars believe their own lies. It is a notable fact that the integrity of mankind is deteriorating at a rapid pace because of demonic influences.

Liars and pretentious individuals are unaware that individuals who are filled with the "Holy Spirit" have the ability to discern falseness. I've talked with many people whom I knew were lying because the **"Holy Spirit"** dwelling inside of me reveals the truth. Liars deceive themselves when communicating with God's children.

The "Falling Away"

There is a popular saying, "A man is only as good as his word." This is a true statement. A liar cannot be relied upon or trusted; and, it is impossible to have a healthy relationship with a liar.

The below scripture confirms that Satan is the father of lies, and that liars are his children. Therefore, contrary to what most say and think, <u>we all are not children of God</u>. Yes, God created all of us, but those who ignore His word and don't acknowledge Him as their heavenly father are not His children.

<u>John 8</u>: "[44]You are of your father the devil, and your will is to do your father's desires. He was a murderer from the beginning, and has nothing to do with the truth, because there is no truth in him. When he lies, he speaks according to his own nature, for he is a liar and the father of lies."

c) **Hands That Shed Innocent Blood:**
   Individual murders and mass murdering is on the rise domestically and internationally.

   - Children are being killed by parents and strangers;

The "Falling Away"

- Children are murdering each other in schools, on the streets (gangs), and murdering their parents;

- Terrorists and hate organizations are killing people because of their ethnicity, religion, and political beliefs;

- Military retaliations in the Middle-East are targeting innocent unarmed people along with their military rivals;

- Strangers killing strangers on public streets and freeways (road rage).

It is God's will for us to love one another and to protect our children. Not so long ago, neighbors knew and respected each other. Today, it is uncommon to know your neighbor. When God says for us to love one another, He means to respect and support each other. People need people. God gives man a free will and does not force any of us to do His will. With the majority of people ignoring God's word, they're becoming vulnerable to the demonic influences of hatred.

I John 4: "(7)Beloved, let us love one another: for love is of God; and every one that loveth is born of God, and knoweth

The "Falling Away"

God. **[8]He that loveth not knoweth not God, for God is love."**

The lack of love (respect and support toward each other) that the world is currently experiencing is metaphorically referred to in Biblical scripture as love being waxed (e.g., immovable – at a stand still). God said this would happen among mankind during the **"Falling Away."**

The below scriptures confirms how the love of many will become less during the last days.

Matthew 24: "[12]And because iniquity shall abound, the love of many shall wax cold."

The increased shedding of innocent blood among families, strangers, and in wars is occurring because the love of many have become wax cold.

God warns us in the below scriptures that the day will come when families will become divided.

Isaiah 1: "[4]Ah sinful nation, a people laden with iniquity, a seed of evildoers, children that are corrupters: they have forsaken the LORD, they have provoked the Holy One of

The "Falling Away"

Israel unto anger, they are gone away backward."

Matthew 10: "[21]Brother will deliver up brother to death, and the father his child, and children will rise against parents and have them put to death."

Ephesians 6: "[4]And, ye fathers provoke not your children to wrath: but bring them up in the nurture and admonition of the Lord."

Proverbs 22: "[6]Train up a child in the way he should go, and when he is old he will not depart from it."

The lack of good training among our children causes criminal behavior. There's an overwhelming increase of children being disobedient to parents and to their teachers. This is especially true for those parents who are involved in sinful lifestyles and are neglecting to properly train their children. Today's generation of disobedient youths is dangerous. They lack knowledge of what's evil and good.

Parents are responsible to train their children what's right and wrong. By doing so, they will mature to become obedient and respectful. Far too many parents are failing to teach their children God's laws. This contributes to lack of knowledge of good and evil. In essence, youths are submissive to whatever is evil and popular in this world; they are unaware of the boundaries between right and wrong.

Demonic influences are causing our legislature to change laws that originated from God's word to accommodate sin. Parents can no longer spank their children. It is considered abuse. Children are being taught to call the police if spanked by a parent. This law is contrary to God's law.

Our children are not being taught God's laws, to respect their elders, others, and themselves. A recent Department of Education survey, which analyzed violence in U.S. schools, reported that public schools nationwide experienced more than 11,000 fights in which weapons were used, 4,000 rapes and other sexual assaults, and 7,000 robberies. The suicide rate among U.S. teens has risen 120% in the last 15 years while drug use has risen almost 80% since 1992.

The Bible tells us about a time when these kind of violent acts will be committed by children all over the world. It's happening now during the **"Falling Away."** Take a look at the following scripture:

Proverbs 30:11-14: "There is a generation that curseth their father, and doth not bless their mother. There is a generation that is pure in their own eyes, and yet is not washed from their filthiness. There is a generation, O how lofty are their eyes! and their eyelids are lifted up. There is a generation, whose teeth are as swords, and their jaw teeth as knives, to devour the poor from off the earth, and the needy from among men."

Today in America, the "antichrist" spirit is increasingly influencing the removal of public recognition of God. This evil influence is responsible for the United States Supreme Court making the decision to remove prayer from schools in 1962. Statistics show that crime, venereal disease, premarital sex, illiteracy, suicide, drug use, public corruption, and other social ills dramatically increased since that time.

Increased killings among family and friends usually occur with unbelievers. Seldom does murdering take place among Christian families and friends. God knows all things. As a child of God, do you think He will allow someone to come into your life knowing that the individual is going to kill you?

It is Satan's goal to kill and destroy mankind. He brings people together, sometimes, for the purpose of murder. Worldly love can be destructive (e.g., it is conditional, can become harmful, deceitful, unreliable, and is often short-term). Think of all the couples that have dated or married, and the relationship ended because one murdered the other.

There is an increase of killings in romantic relationships. Know that God has nothing to do with these people coming together. When God brings a couple together, no man can cause separation. Godly love is unconditional, monogamous, joyful, long lasting, patient, peaceful, protective, and reliable.

Christians love their spouses as they love themselves. Murders seldom take place with these couples compared to those who don't practice Christianity or know God.

In the below scriptures, God commands husbands to love (be faithful and honor) their wives and for wives to be subject (submissive) to their husbands. The wife is to be available to help and please the husband. God is not asking. He ordains this commandment of love for Christian couples. There is no scripture in the Bible where God says wives are to love their husbands because His special anointed influence makes it happen.

Husbands:
Colossians 3: "[19]Husbands love your wives, and do not be harsh with them."

Ephesians 5: "[25]Husbands love your wives, as Christ loved the church and gave himself up for her."

Ephesians 5: "[28]Even so husbands should love their wives as their own bodies. He who loves his wife loves himself."

The Wives:
Ephesians 5: "[22]Wives be subject to your husbands, as to the Lord."

Ephesians 5: "[24]As the church is subject to Christ, so let wives also be subject in everything to their husbands."

I reiterate that marriages are vulnerable to adultery, disrespect, emotional and physical abuse, lies, and murder when God is not the head of the union.

d) **A Heart That Devises Wicked Imaginations.** These people are influenced by demons, and some are possessed by them. Wicked imaginations are being introduced to people via magazines, movies, TV, and the internet. These resources are channeling perverted imaginations to adults and children. There are more movies and television sitcoms being produced that are about murders, werewolves, zombies, sex, and witches than there are positive ones. It is sad to say that these shows are popular to the majority. What does this say about mankind's state of mind?

I recently saw a video online of nude men and women urinating in each other's mouths while indulging in sex. How could that possibly be enjoyable? Satan definitely inspires one to have sex in painful and unhealthy ways. There are no limits to these wicked imaginations that are increasingly influencing people. God says in His word that there would be **INCONTINENCE** (no control over sexual appetites) during the **"Falling Away."** It's definitely happening notoriously right now.

II Timothy 1-3: **"(1)This know also, that in the last days perilous times shall come. (2) For men shall be lovers of their own selves, covetous, boasters, proud, blasphemers,**

disobedient to parents, unthankful, unholy, [3]Without natural affection, trucebreakers, false accusers, <u>incontinent (lacking restraint in sexual matters)</u>, fierce, despisers of those that are good."

e) **Feet that be Swift in Running to Mischief:**
    Being mischievous is a troublemaker or a wrong doer who is commonly known as a low life. Feet that are swift in running to mischief mean anyone who is ready and willing to do evil. The world is becoming a very dangerous and precarious place because of mischievous people. Without hesitation or remorse, crimes and unbelievable sinful acts are occurring throughout the world.

    I Peter 4: "[15]But let none of you suffer as a murderer, or a thief, or a wrong doer, or as a busybody in other men's matters."

f) **False Witness:**
    A false witness is someone who lies in giving account for hearing or seeing evidence of a situation.

g) **Soweth Discord Among Brethren:**
    This means one who is a backbiter (to make spiteful comments about someone who is not present), gossiper, responsible for causing

The "Falling Away"

anger and volatile relationships among others, and betraying one's trust.

Matthew 24: "**(10)And then many will fall away, and betray one another, and hate one another.**

I John 4: "**(20)If any one says, I love God, and hates his brother, he is a liar; for he who does not love his brother whom he has seen, cannot love God whom he has not seen.**"

God says in His word that during the **"Falling Away,"** the above sinful characteristics would increase among mankind. Wouldn't you say that it's happening now?

The "Falling Away"

Chapter Five
Having Their Consciences Seared With a Hot Iron (No Guilt – No Remorse)

Today, most of us are traumatized by hideous increased crimes that are being committed throughout the world without remorse. We ask, "How can human beings do such things?" According to Biblical scripture, when the conscience is seared, burned out, people become like wild animals in their behavior.

The below scripture clearly states that during the **"Falling Away,"** many will no longer have a conscience to have regrets. Metaphorically, it describes the conscience as being seared with a hot iron – burnt away.

I Timothy 4: "[1]Now the Spirit speaketh expressly, that in the latter times some shall depart from the faith, giving heed to seducing spirits, and doctrines of devils; [2]Speaking lies in hypocrisy; having their conscience seared with a hot iron."

Because of the existing spiritual warfare, it is very important for Christians to allow the conscience to become renewed to reflect God's standards. In other words, study God's word and obey it. There are Biblical scriptures pertaining to every aspect of our lives.

The "Falling Away"

Increased Killings, no Conscience or Remorse:
It is impossible for the media to report all increased crimes that are occurring. However, the fact that they are occurring is evident that the conscience of many no longer exist.

Increase of Corporate Crimes – No Remorse:
There is an increase of fraudulent corporate crimes being committed by corporate executives throughout the United States that will eventually bring about destructive devastation for many. The primary cause of these crimes is GREED. Recently, there have been merges taking place for survival purposes between major corporations, including banks, and numerous reports about fraudulent CEOs. Greed is destructive and is the primary cause of many corporations' demise.

In addition to greed, there are many other factors contributing to corporate failures throughout America and the world. I'm convinced that disobedience to God's word pertaining to how employees are treated has much to do with increased corporate failure. There are numerous illegal practices that are directed towards African-Americans and other minorities in American corporations. It is a known fact that African-Americans' salaries are lower than Caucasians, there are less opportunities for promotions, and they are the first to be layed off regardless of education and tenure. There is a significant increase of unemployment among African-Americans throughout America. There is a major decline of African-Americans being employed in corporations. Statistics reveals that it is 90% less compared to the 1960s, 1970s, and 1980s when corporate employees consisted of all ethnicities.

What I'm about to say may be somewhat surprising. There is a universal law derived from biblical scripture that says, **"What you sow you reap,"** meaning **"What goes around must come around."** God warns us in His word for **employers** to be fair and respectful to their employees because He is watching.

Colossians 4: "[1]Masters (employers) give unto your servants (employees) that which is just and equal; knowing that ye also have a Master in Heaven."

Ephesians 6: "[9]And, ye masters (employers) do the same things unto them (employees), forbearing threatening: knowing that your master also is in heaven; neither is there respect of persons with him."

It is God's law that employers treat their employees fairly, and for employees to perform their jobs to the best of their ability and to respect their employers. Disobedience to the above can result in serious consequences such as FAILURE.

The "Falling Away"

In the world today, corporate management has become cut-throat and have no remorse.

The following is an experience I encountered while working at a major corporation.

I accepted a position as an Executive Assistant in the executive office of a major corporation. The office manager, who recommended me for the position, ignored me as though I was invisible. The executive officer, who hired me, communicated with me only when it was necessary and was very talkative to others. I was very uncomfortable working in this humiliating environment. Daily, I asked God why was I there? Months went by before I heard from the Lord. After working at this corporation for one year, the Lord spoke to me and said *"I'm with you, wait and watch."*

I began to notice the following unfair practices that were being directed toward employees. They were the opposite of God's word.

- **The CEO and his officers were high minded and had no respect for the executive office staff.**

- **Huge financial bonuses were distributed among the officers, and the staff who supported them received nothing.**

- Salary Discrimination - newly hired Caucasian employees were paid more than African-American employees who had seniority and same position.

- African-Americans were the first to be layed off vs. newly hired Caucasians regardless of seniority.

- To afford paying overtime, employees with low salaries were classified as salaried vs. hourly pay.

Finally, the time was near for me to leave the company. The Lord spoke to me again and said, "The Corporation's stock was going to become worthless, that the CEO and all the officers would be terminated by Board." He instructed me to reschedule my surgery and to have it within 30 days so that my insurance covers it, and that He was removing me from the job." I obeyed and made arrangements for my surgery to take place within several weeks.

While, at home recuperating from surgery, the Board terminated the CEO and the officers because of mismanaged funds. The stock decreased enormously in value and became worthless. I asked God what was the purpose of my knowing these things before they happened. He told me that it was necessary for me to see His wrath upon the evil doers who had victimized His children. He told me that I questioned whether He was with me because of the difficulty that I was experiencing, and He wanted me to know that He is true to His word and that no weapon formed against me could prosper. My faith became stronger after this ordeal.

Employers don't realize that God is very much concerned about relationships between the employee and employer. He clearly states in His word that He watches over His children (believers) in all things. No one can escape from God's wrath that is responsible for afflicting His children. God is a God of love and Vengeance. Unfortunately, unfair managers don't realize that when they mistreat employees who are believers, they're taking on a battle directly with God.

Romans 13: "[(4)]**For he is the minister of God to thee for good. But if thou do that which is evil, be afraid; for he beareth not the sword in vain: for he is the minister of God, a revenger to execute wrath upon him that doeth evil.**"

The "Falling Away"

Chapter Six
Forbidding to Marry
(Fornication)

In America, fornication is no longer considered a forbidden behavior. In the churches, "houses of worship", there are many engaged couples who think they're Christians while living together as though they're already married. Being engaged doesn't validate living in sin. Unmarried couples living together as husband and wife are disobeying the word of God. Metaphorically, "cohabiting" is very much like being trapped in a **"Black Widow's Web."** Love has nothing to do with the majority of men living with women in uncommitted relationships. Convenience is the primary purpose of "cohabiting." What men don't realize is that God created women to have a strong influence over them. There have been men, called by God, who were empowered with extraordinary gifts. They became weak and destroyed by getting involved with the wrong woman (e.g., Samson and King Solomon). Therefore, it behooves men and women not to get involved with someone they don't want a commitment with or who is unequally yoked (not mentally and spiritually on the same path).

Marriage is ordained by God and is considered honorable. What makes a man and woman become husband and wife in the eyes of God is not the marriage license; that's the law of this world. **It is the vows that are made before God between a man and woman to love and honor until death. Once sexual consummation takes place between the couple, they become one flesh (husband and wife). Making a vow(s) to God is serious. He hears and holds us accountable to our vows.**

Ephesians 5: "**(31)For this cause, shall a man leave his father and mother, <u>and shall be joined unto his wife, and they two shall be one flesh.</u>**"

Psalms 61: "**(5)<u>For thou, O God, hast heard my vows</u>: thou hast given me the heritage of those that fear thy name.**"

Ecclesiastes 5: "**(5)<u>Better is it that thou should not vow, than that thou shouldest vow and not pay (honor).</u>**"

The majority of women are "cohabiting" with the intent of sedulously getting men to marry them.

Achieving something good, by doing wrong, is never long lasting. If "cohabiting" develops into a marriage, most likely it will be an entrapment of misery because it came about the wrong way.

This is a legitimate warning to those who are in love and plan to marry. Do not consider "cohabiting." No one benefits from disobeying God's laws.

It is not Satan's desire for man and woman to be together as husband and wife or as lovers. He prefers homosexual relationships. Therefore, when demonic influences entice couples to live together in sin, be assured that at least eight out of ten of these relationships will <u>not</u> result in marriage. The few that marry will be at high risk of experiencing various kinds of misery. There will be a lack of trust, and a multitude of unrealistic fears that will keep them bound together – trapped for the sake of being miserable.

Remember, it is not Satan's desire that we be happy. His job is to deceive and destroy us in any way that he can.

<u>Proverbs 18</u>: "[22]Whoso findeth a wife, findeth a good thing, and obtaineth favor of the Lord."

<u>1 Corinthians 7</u>: "[2]Nevertheless, to avoid fornication, let every man have his own wife, and let every woman have her own husband."

<u>I Timothy 5</u>: "[6]But she that lives in pleasure is dead (spiritually dead) while she lives."

Scriptures confirm that men and women living in disobedience to God's word by surrendering to the lusts of their flesh are **spiritually dead and are disconnected from God.** They're on the path to eternal death.

I reiterate that abstaining from marrying and living together in sin is a serious offense to God. Although the relationship may begin blissfully, the relationship often times result in a horrific experience even if it develops into a marriage.

If you are a believer of Christ, then living in sin should not have a place in your life. Christians are to be witnesses to others. We cannot disobey the laws of God without hindering others from coming to Christ. We must live our lives in obedience before a sinful and wicked world.

I Corinthians 6: **"(13)Meats for the belly, and the belly for meats: but God shall destroy both it and them. <u>Now the body is not for fornication</u>, but for the Lord: and the Lord for the body. (14) And God hath both raised up the Lord, and will also raise up us by his own power. (15) Know ye not that your bodies are the members of Christ? Shall I then take the members of Christ, and make them the members of a harlot? God forbid. (16)What? <u>Know ye not that he which is joined to a harlot is one body? For two saith he, shall be one flesh.</u> (17)But, he that is joined unto the Lord is one spirit. (18)Flee fornication. Every sin that a**

man doeth is without the body (the body of Christ – the Church); <u>but he that committeth fornication sinneth against his own body.</u> ⁽¹⁹⁾What? Now ye not that your body is the temple of the "Holy Ghost" which is in you, which ye have of God, and <u>ye are not your own?</u> ⁽²⁰⁾For ye are bought with a price: therefore, glorify God in your body, and in your spirit, which are God's."

<u>I Corinthians 7:</u> "⁽⁹⁾But if they cannot contain, let them marry: for it is better to marry than to burn."

<u>Isaiah 55:</u> "<u>⁽⁸⁾For my thoughts are not your thoughts, neither are your ways my ways, saith the LORD. ⁽⁹⁾ Or as the heavens are higher than the earth, so are my ways higher than your ways, and my thoughts than your thoughts.</u>"

As Christians, we cannot think like God until we become knowledgeable of His word. Even then, we all fall short.

<u>Isaiah 55:</u> "⁽⁷⁾Let the wicked forsake his way, and the unrighteous man his thoughts: and let him return unto the LORD, and he will have mercy upon him; and to our God, for he will abundantly pardon."

The "Falling Away"

I Corinthians 6: "**(13)** **Now the body is not for fornication**, but for the Lord: and the Lord for the body.**

Sex should be considered private, sacred, and for the enjoyment of the husband and wife <u>only</u>. Consider the fact that if sex were only between married couples, there would be no sexual related diseases in the world today.

Romans 12: "**(2)**And, be not conformed to this world: but be ye transformed by the renewing of your mind (study God's word) that ye may prove what is that good, and acceptable and perfect will of God.**"

Proverbs 28: "**(9)**He that turneth his ear from hearing the law, even his prayer shall be abomination.**"

Unfortunately, sinners who pray to God do not know the above scripture. This particular scripture is clearly saying that when you're living in disobedience, the only prayer heard by God from you is one asking for sincere forgiveness. In other words, one cannot deliberately be disobedient and expect blessings from God. Far too many people are praying to God while practicing sinful lifestyles. When sinners' prayers are answered, Satan is the one answering those prayers; thereby, deceiving sinners that it is the true God.

The "Falling Away"

Therefore, sinners are deceived by thinking that their lifestyles are acceptable to God because they believe that He's answering their prayers.

Regardless of how sinful a lifestyle may be, God has the desire and power to deliver anyone who asks. He is a forgiving God and loves us all. God gives us a free will to choose right or wrong. We are not robots. Sin is what separates us from God, because He cannot be in its presence. He gave His only son to save us from eternal death. Disbelief and spiritual deceit has a lot to do with many choosing the way of sin.

It is impossible for anyone to stop practicing sin without the help of God, because we all are natural born sinners. To become Christ-like, we must allow God to be the potter and we become the clay. After all, He's the Creator.

Romans 6: "(23)For the wages of sin is death; but the gift of God is eternal life through Jesus Christ our Lord."

The "Falling Away"

Chapter Seven
Abstaining From Eating Meats

In the beginning of creation, all of God's creations including animals were vegetarians. God spoke the below to Adam and Eve in the Garden of Eden:

Genesis 1:29-30: **"I give you every seed-bearing plant on the face of the whole earth and every tree that has fruit with seed in it. They will be food for you. And to the beasts of the earth and all the birds of the air and all the creatures that move on the ground--everything that has the breath of life in it -I give every green plant for food. And it was so."**

It wasn't until after the waters of the "Great Flood" receded and Noah and his family were left to replenish the earth when God gave permission for mankind to eat meat.

Genesis 9: **"[1] Then God blessed Noah and his sons, saying to them, "Be fruitful and increase in number and fill the earth. [2]The fear and dread of you will fall upon all of the beasts of the earth and all the birds of the air, <u>upon every creature that moves along the ground, and upon all the fish of the sea; they are given into your hands. [3]Everything that lives and**

**moves will be food for you. Just as I gave you
the green plants, now I give you everything."**

Today, we often hear that meat is unhealthy to be
eaten. Within the last thirty years, many people
have abstained from eating meats due to this
belief. Doctors and dietitians advocate that being
a vegetarian is healthier. When I was a child, it
was rare to not include meat with meals.
Abstaining from eating meats is a demonic
influence because it's contrary to God's word. I'm
not saying that it is evil not to eat meat. We have a
free will to eat whatever we desire. However,
according to the Bible, there is nothing unhealthy
about eating meats. God says that all meats are to
be eaten (can be eaten) with thanksgiving. In other
words, when you bless or pray over your food, it
supernaturally becomes blessed food and cannot
hurt you. Also, He says that all meats are created
by Him and are good to be eaten.

With God being omnipotent, He knew the day
would come when food and water would be
chemically processed – unhealthy. Therefore, He
provided us with the benefit of blessing our food
by praying over it. Many people are unable to eat
certain foods without becoming ill because they
don't bless their foods.

I Timothy 4: **"⁽⁴⁾For every creature of God is
good and nothing to be refused, if it be received**

with thanksgiving.[5]<u>For it is sanctified by the word of God and prayer.</u>"

Believing that vegetables are healthier than meats is a lie that's being spiritually influenced among mankind. All foods eaten are chemically processed. Fruit and vegetable seeds are planted in toxic soil and fertilization that has chemicals. Once the fruit and vegetables begin to mature, they are sprayed with chemicals. The livestock and poultry that we eat are fed chemicals to prevent diseases. The same applies to the water that we drink. Advertisements stating that certain foods are organic may not necessarily be true. Perhaps there are some foods that are organic, but how do you know? For healthy purposes, all food should be blessed prior to eating.

<u>I Corinthians 8</u>: "[8]But meat commendeth us not to God: for neither, if we eat, are we the better; neither, if we eat not, are we the worse."

<u>Colossians 2</u>: "[16]Let no man therefore judge you in meat, or in drink, or in respect of a holy day, or of the new moon, or of the Sabbath days."

We are to respect those who look at certain meats as holy and not offend our fellow man by eating these meats in their presence.

The "Falling Away"

I Corinthians 8: "[13]Wherefore, if meat make my brother to offend, I will eat no flesh while the world standeth, lest I make my brother to offend."

Romans 14: "[2]One man's faith allows him to eat everything, but another man, whose faith is weak, eats only vegetables. [3]The man who eats everything must not look down on him who does not, and the man who does not eat everything must not condemn the man who does, for God has accepted him."

Whatever you believe is what you receive. Whatever you expect is what you get. This is a universal law. Who are we to believe the creator or man? As a believer of God's unchanging word, I believe that we can eat whatever we desire as long as we bless it. Christians are a peculiar people with supernatural abilities that God empowers them with through the Holy Spirit.

Mark 16: "[17]And these signs shall follow them that believe; in my name shall they cast out devils, they shall speak with new tongues; [18]they shall take up serpents; and if they drink any deadly thing, it shall not hurt them; they shall lay hands on the sick, and they shall recover. [19] So then after the Lord had spoken unto them, he was received up into heaven, and sat on the right hand of God, the Father."

The "Falling Away"

Chapter Eight
Perilous Times Shall Come

Perverted lifestyles and violence throughout the world during the days of Noah that caused the earth to be destroyed by water are similar to perilous conditions that are developing today throughout the world. The omission of God in our laws and lifestyles are opening spiritual doors for evil to revisit the world in a manner that mankind has never seen. Since the majority of people are spiritually disconnected from God, their ears are deaf and eyes are blind to the spiritual devastations that are already present among us. Biblical scripture refer to this condition as **"the beginning of sorrows"**.

II Chronicles 7: **"[14]If my people who are called by my name humble themselves, and pray and seek my face, and turn from their wicked ways, then I will hear from heaven, and will forgive their sin and heal their land."**

It would be great if mankind would repent throughout the world. However, I doubt that this will ever occur because most are offended by the mention of God; and, far too many Christians are rebellious against reproof of sin. Our laws have executed the removal of acknowledging God or having prayer in our public schools.

The "Falling Away"

The world was a much safer place to live 50 years ago. Security bars and burglar alarms for private businesses, homes, and automobiles were not necessary or owned by most people. During the night, people living in rural areas or small towns would sleep with their windows opened during the summer. There was no fear of theft when leaving keys in a parked automobile. People were able to walk or drive down a public street without fearing attacks or getting shot. Children could play outside without supervision or fear of abductions. Those days are far gone.

The world is no longer at peace domestically or internationally. Whatever crime you can imagine, no matter how gruesome, it exists.

With the current chaos in America, the **"New War"** against terrorists appears to be escalating in the Middle East.

II Timothy 3: **"[1]This know also, that in the last days perilous times shall come."**

When Christ was here, the disciples asked Him what shall be the signs of His coming for the Church (believers) and the end of time. Jesus responded as shown in the below scriptures.

Matthew 24: **"[3]And as he sat upon the Mount of Olives, the disciples came unto him privately,**

saying, tell us, when shall these things be? And what shall be the <u>sign of thy coming</u>, and of the <u>end of the world</u>? [4]And Jesus answered and said unto him, take heed that no man deceives you. [5]<u>For many shall come in my name, saying, I am Christ; and shall deceive many</u>.

[6]<u>And ye shall hear of wars and rumors of wars</u>: see that ye be not troubled: for all these things must come to pass, but the end is not yet. [7]<u>For nation shall rise against nation, and kingdom against kingdom: and there shall be famines, and pestilences, and earthquakes, in divers places</u>. [8]<u>All these are the "BEGINNING OF SORROWS"</u>. [9]<u>Then shall they deliver you to be afflicted. and shall kill you (CHRISTIANS): and ye shall be hated of all nations for my name's sake. These are the beginning of sorrows</u>. [10]<u>And then shall many be offended, and shall betray one another, and shall hate one another.</u> [11]<u>And many false prophets shall rise, and shall deceive many.</u> [12]<u>And because iniquity shall abound, the love of many shall wax cold</u>. [13]But he that shall endure unto the end, the same shall be saved. [14]And this gospel of the kingdom shall be preached in all the world for a witness unto all nations; <u>and then shall the end come.</u> [15]When ye therefore shall see the "<u>Abomination of Desolation</u>," spoken of by Daniel the prophet, stand in the holy place, (whoso readeth, let him understand)[16]Then let them which be in Judea

flee into the mountains: [17]Let him which is on the housetop not come down to take any thing out of his house: [18]Neither let him which is in the field return back to take his clothes. [19]And woe unto them that are with child and to them that give suck in those days! [20]But pray ye that your flight be not in the winter, neither on the Sabbath day: [21]For then shall be great tribulation, such as was not since the beginning of the world to this time, no, nor ever shall be. [22]And except those days should be shortened, there should no flesh be saved: <u>but for the elect's sake (Christians) those days shall be shortened (Rapture will take place)</u>. [23]Then if any man shall say unto you, Lo, here is Christ, or there, believe it not. [24]For there shall arise false Christs (Son-of-Satan), and false prophets, and shall show great signs and wonders; insomuch that, if it were possible, they shall deceive the very elect."

The below scriptures are referenced in the above, Matthew Chapter 24:

<u>Scriptures 3-9</u> describe the **"<u>Beginning of Sorrows</u>"** that began in the late 1970s. See below specifics:

• False prophets will come in the name of Christ deceiving many. **This is happening now**. In 1978, a well known false prophet, Jim Jones, was the founder (in 1950) and leader of "The Peoples Temple. I remember (late 1960's) the church where I grew up worshipping, took a bus filled with members to visit the Temple in San Francisco. Jim Jones was prophesying and performing miracles like no one else. He was deceiving many Christians. The day finally came when the world saw clearly that he was a false prophet. He led his adult followers to a mass murder suicide in Georgetown, Guyana. Nearly 300 children were murdered by cyanide poisoning. Jones died from a gunshot wound to the head. It is suspected his death was suicide. **There are many false prophets in existence today.**

- There will be wars and rumors of wars. **The world has been experiencing numerous wars since Vietnam in the late 1960s to the present.**

- Nations shall rise against nations and kingdoms against kingdoms. **This is currently happening.**

- There shall be famines, and pestilences, and earthquakes in different places. **This is currently happening**.

- Christians will be afflicted, killed, and hated in all nations. It was recently reported on the news that there is an increase of Christians being killed. **This is currently happening and increasing.**

The above is occurring in Africa, China, North Korea, Pakistan, Palestine, Saudi Arabia and other places where Christianity is not the prevailing faith. Eventually, Christian killings will take place within the U.S.A. With the possibility of terrorist cells being here, **"Suicide Bombers"** can declare war at any time. The antichrist spirit is already present.

<u>Scriptures 13-14</u> says that during the **"Falling Away,"** evil influences will cause many Christians to become unsaved. Those who will remain obedient to God's laws during these deceiving and perilous times shall be saved. **This is already happening with the Church. Most Christians are not worshipping God in spirit and truth. They have fallen away to self-righteousness, false teachings because of demonic influences.** Also, the gospel of the kingdom must be preached in the entire world for a witness unto all nations. This is happening now through missionaries and television.

The **"Beginning of Sorrows"** is evident today. The **"Falling Away"** epoch in <u>Scriptures 10-12</u> became visible to me in the mid-1980s and is rapidly escalating with the **"new war" against terrorists that began in October 2001. I believe future wars against terrorists will bring about the beginning of the "ABOMINATION OF DESOLATION" that is referred to in** <u>Scripture 15</u>. <u>Scriptures 16-20</u> specifically states that during the destructive war, regardless of where you are or what you're doing, find protection – forget about anything else. This scripture is referring to "weapons of mass destruction."

I strongly believe that attacking Iraq will open doors for all other nations in the Middle East to eventually go to war. This will, eventually, bring about the **"Abomination of Desolation" that is referenced in Scripture 15.** This war will destroy many civilian and military lives, and leave the whole world experiencing a **"Tribulation"** that it has never known since the beginning of time. During this time, it will be mandatory to have a **worldwide leader** who can bring peace, stabilize and refurbish worldwide nations. This brilliant leader will appear to have all of the right answers as well as supernatural powers. The world will be accepting and astonished at his ingenuity. He will disguise himself as a peacemaker; **HE WILL BE THE "ANTICHRIST."**

<u>Scripture 21</u> refers to the **"Tribulation"** that follows the War.

The "Falling Away"

Scripture 22 says that the **"Tribulation"** is going to be so devastating that, hopefully, the Christians' days will be short, referring to the **"Rapture" (when Christ comes for the church aka Christians to meet Him in the air).**

Scriptures 23-24 says that during the **"Tribulation,"** there will be a false Christ and false prophets showing great signs and wonders. Many, including Christians, will believe that the worldwide leader is Christ. God warns us about being deceived by them. He is referring to the **"Antichrist"** who will come with great signs and wonders.

I Thessalonians 4: **"[17]Then we who are alive, who are left, shall be caught up together with them in the clouds to meet the Lord in the air; and so we shall always be with the Lord."**

Christ is going to remove His Church (Christians) from this world during the **"Tribulation"** that will last for seven years. During this time, the **"Antichrist"** will be persecuting Christians throughout the world in ways that will be unimaginable. Many theologians think that it will last for seven years and that the **"Rapture"** will take place during the first three and a half (3-1/2) years, and some think that the **"Rapture"** will take place at the end of the seven (7) years.

95

The "Falling Away"

I believe the **"Rapture"** will take place sometime during the first three and a half (3 ½) years after the **"Antichrist"** is revealed. During the last three and a half (3-1/2) years is when Moses and Elijah will return to witness (**Revelations 11:3-7**), and then **"The End"** of the world as we know it will come at the end of the "Antichrist's" seven (7) year reign.

Chapter Nine
Men Shall be Lovers of Their Own Selves

Today, homosexual lifestyles are gaining rapid acceptance and increasing indulgence among mankind regardless of religious belief, gender, or racial ethnicity. **God is the only creator of mankind. He does not create anyone destined to go to hell.** Contrary to the carnal thinking of man, no one is born into this world as a homosexual. This is what Satan wants people to believe, and he is a liar.

Adultery, fornication, pornography, and other sexual perversions open doors for Satan to influence mankind with the abominable spirit of homosexuality. For example, when a heterosexual man has sex with two lesbian women, this act summons spiritual influences of homosexuality to take control of influencing him. In other words, people can become homosexuals when they yield to unnatural sexual acts or lusts.

Homosexuality is considered an abomination to God because it is unnatural. It also brings death to the spirit of man and disconnects him from God.

Leviticus 18: **"(22)Thou shalt not lie with mankind as with womankind. It is an abomination."**

The "Falling Away"

Leviticus 20: "**(13)If a man also lie with mankind, as he lieth with a woman, both of them have committed an abomination: they shall surely be put to death; their blood shall be upon them.**"

I Corinthians 6: "**(9)Know ye not that the unrighteous shall not inherit the kingdom of God? Be not deceived: neither fornicators, nor idolaters, nor adulterers, nor effeminate (homosexuals), nor abusers of themselves with mankind.**"

Satan is the creator of homosexual desires. During ancient times, he spiritually influenced homosexuality among all of the Canaanites (including children) in Sodom and Gomorrah. These two cities were located in the eastern plains of Jordan. This evil lifestyle was widespread among all of the people in these two cities with the exception of Lot and his family. God sent two angels to escort Lot and his family from the city of Sodom before he destroyed both cities and all of the homosexuals with fire from heaven.

Genesis 19: "**(1)And there came two angels to Sodom at evening; and Lot sat in the gate of Sodom: and Lot seeing them rose up to meet them; and he bowed himself with his face toward the ground.**"

After Lot and his family left the city, Lot saw (below scripture):

Genesis 19: "**[28]And he looked toward Sodom and Gomorrah, and toward all the land of the plain, and beheld, and, lo, the smoke of the country went up as the smoke of a furnace.**"

The word sodomy originates from the city, Sodom. During these ancient times, the law in Sodom and Gomorrah was to perform <u>anal penetration</u> with every stranger that entered the two cities for the purposes of asserting control and pleasure; a practice that is very much alive in our prisons today for that very same purpose – to conquer and to control another.

Frequently Spoken Statement and Question: I knew that I was a homosexual when I was a teenager. I did everything to become interested in the opposite sex and could not. I was born a homosexual. If God didn't intend for me to be this way, why am I?

Answer:
One becomes a homosexual because of demonic influences of the mind or demonic possession of the body. These spiritual influences will attack anyone regardless of age, ethnicity, gender or religion. In many cases, homosexual demons begin influencing a child at an early age. Parents

who lack knowledge that homosexuality is an attack from Satan, accepts the lie that their child is born this way. Acceptance is the operative word. When adults and youths believe that they're born homosexuals, they'll live their lives as such without any attempts to change. Unfortunately, they are being deceived by the father of lies, Satan.

When Christian parents, who are knowledgeable of God's word, observe that their child is being attacked by a homosexual spiritual influence, they have this spirit rebuked from their child by a "Holy-Ghost" filled Pastor or Christian. God's word is the **only POWER** that can defeat Satan's attacks. I believe another reason an innocent child is spiritually influenced to go the wrong way is because of the parent's disobedience. According to scripture, when parents are obedient to God's word, it is confirmed that the child will be blessed. This does not mean that the child will be exempt from spiritual attacks.

Deuteronomy 28: "[4]Blessed shall be the fruit of thy body (children)."

When parents are disobedient, ignoring God's ways, it is confirmed that the child will be cursed. **Deuteronomy 28 "[18]Cursed shall be the fruit of thy body (children)."**

However, if a child from a curse womb becomes of age, knowledgeable of God's word, and accepts the Lord as "Savior", he or she becomes blessed, a new creature, and old things are passed away. If asked, God will free anyone from Satan's traps.

We all have the same opportunities of becoming a new creature in Christ whether we are born from a blessed or cursed womb because everyone is born a sinner.

In <u>Hebrews 4:12,</u> scripture clearly states that God's word is a WEAPON against Satanic powers. As a believer and doer, we don't have to ACCEPT any sickness, sinful desires or thoughts that Satan brings our way.

<u>**There are two kinds of homosexuals:**</u>
a) **<u>Bisexuals</u>** are homosexuals whose minds are demonically influenced to have sexual lusts for men and women. Most bisexual men and women are deceiving and don't want the opposite sex to know about their sexual desires. <u>It is their minds that are influenced by Satan – not demon possession</u>. Many bisexuals are married to the opposite sex and have children; the majorities are in the closet about their homosexual desires and acts. This kind of deceit exposes the spouse to life-threatening diseases.

Seven years ago during Christmas time, the news reported a police raid that took place at a shopping center in northern California, where homosexual solicitations and sexual acts were taking place for several weeks in a restroom at a public park. Approximately thirty men were arrested. The shocking news was that twenty of them were married to women. Can you imagine how the wives felt when they learned that their husbands were homosexuals?

b) **Gays and Lesbians**: They are demon possessed. Gay men lust for the same sex only. They have feminine characteristics and think a female spirit lives within. Lesbians lust for the same sex only. These women portray masculine characteristics in their behavior and thoughts. They believe a male spirit lives within.

There is an enormous increase of transgender surgeries being performed in the world today. Often times, these surgeries make it impossible to determine the true gender. Physicians who specialize in transforming men and women into the opposite sex will one day be required to answer to God for this evil creation.

Spiritual homosexual warfare against heterosexual marriages is on the rise causing couples to divorce and become partners with the same sex. This is becoming very common in our society today. Our youths are being influenced because of the high visibility of homosexuality that is everywhere. Visit school campuses and observe for yourself how our children of all ages are boldly portraying homosexual characteristics. This is frightening.

Below are biblical scriptures pertaining to this sexual abomination:

Romans 1: "**(21)After God had delivered the Israelites out of bondage, they were not thankful but became vain in their imaginations, and their foolish heart was darkened. (24)God gave them up to <u>uncleanness</u> <u>through the lusts of their own hearts to dishonor their own bodies between themselves;</u> (25)<u>Who changed the truth of God into a lie, and worshipped and served the Creature (Satan) more than the Creator, who is blessed forever.</u> Amen (26)For this cause God gave them up unto <u>vile affections:</u> <u>for even their women did change the natural use into that which is against nature:</u> (27)and <u>likewise also the men, leaving the natural use of the woman, burned in their lust one toward another; men with men working that which is unseemly and receiving in themselves that recompense of their error which was met.</u> (28)And even as they did not like to retain God in their knowledge, God gave them over to a <u>reprobate mind to do those things which are not convenient.</u>"**

The "Falling Away"

The above scriptures clearly reveals how God feels about this lifestyle. It is an abomination (vile), unclean and unnatural. One of Satan's primary duties is to influence man to do the opposite of what God says. God created the rectum to release toxic waste from the body not for sexual pleasures. **Sexual anal penetration is unclean, unhealthy, inconvenient, and painful**. Satan's wicked imagination has taken sex, one of the most beautiful pleasures between a man and woman, and turned it into something vile. Satan is very good at deceiving many to believe that God is responsible for the evils that he creates. Homosexuality is not of God.

Regardless of today's acceptance and indulgence of this vile lifestyle, God is not changing His mind or His word pertaining to homosexuality. I can assure you that God's future wrath will be much more disastrous than the destruction of Sodom and Gomorrah. The world is currently plagued with the deadly disease of AIDS that originates from practicing homosexuality.

<u>Psalms 89</u>: "[34]My covenant will I not break, nor alter the thing that is gone out of my lips."

After talking with several bisexuals, I learned that they became that way by getting high at a party and indulging in orgies. It is common for demonic influences to take control when one isn't sober.

The "Falling Away"

This is one of the reasons why God warns against becoming drunk or high by drinking in excess or indulging in drugs.

I Peter 5: "**[8]Be sober, be vigilant; because your adversary the devil, as a roaring lion, walks about, seeking whom he may devour.**"

God loves all people. It is their unnatural SINFUL lifestyle that He hates. He did not create a person to naturally do that which He says is <u>not natural</u>. None of us would be here if God would have created only homosexuals. These couples cannot produce life just like Satan. Why are our laws allowing homosexual couples to adopt innocent children? Isn't it a fact that children mimic their parents? This is another demonic influence that's affecting our law makers.

Thanks to the heavenly father for sending His son, Jesus Christ, who not only created us but who also became man and redeemed us by the shedding of His blood. God can and will deliver anyone from a sinful life. A sinner can become a new creature by studying and obeying God's WORD as the TRUTH and the WAY.

II Corinthians 5: "**[17]Therefore if any man be in Christ, he is a new creature: old things are passed away, behold all things are become new.**"

We don't have to accept or be in bondage to any perverted lifestyle that is influenced by Satan. If anyone falls into Satan's snares, Jesus Christ will set you free if you ask Him.

<u>Isaiah 54</u>: **"(17)No weapon that is formed against thee shall prosper; and every tongue that shall rise against thee in judgment thou shalt condemn. This is the heritage of the servants of the Lord and their righteousness is of me, saith the Lord."**

The below scripture metaphorically depicts God's plan for mankind.

<u>Matthew 13</u>: **"(38)The field is the world; the good seed are the children of the kingdom of God; but the tares are the children of the wicked one; (39)The enemy that sowed them is the devil; the harvest is the end of the world; and the reapers are the angels. (40)As therefore the tares are gathered and burned in the fire; so shall it be in the end of this world. (41)The Son of Man, Christ, shall send forth his angels, and they shall gather out of his kingdom all things that offend, and them which do iniquity; (42)And shall cast them into a furnace of fire: there shall be wailing and gnashing of teeth. (43) Then shall the righteous shine forth as the sun in the Kingdom of their Father. <u>Who hath ears to hear, let him hear.</u>"**

The "Falling Away"

In order to be able to stand against the demonic attacks of Satan, God has equipped us with His word that is a weapon, and with His "Holy Spirit" to lead and guide us.

Hebrew 4: "[12]**For the word of God is quick, and powerful, and sharper than any two edged sword, piercing even to the dividing asunder of soul and spirit, and of the joints and marrow, and is a discerner of the thoughts and intents of the heart.**"

God has equipped His Church, the believers and doers of His word, with the **"Amour of God."** The below scriptures explains that mankind's enemy, Satan and his demons are spirits, describes the **AMOUR** that Christians are to wear, and that the **ONLY WEAPON** that can be used to fight Satan is **THE WORD OF GOD**. Remember, that God and His word are one. God's word will not return unto Him void of power when it is spoken by His children. Wherever it goes, it will accomplish what it is suppose to do.

Ephesians 6: "[11]**Put on the whole Amour of God, that ye may be able to stand against the wiles (attacks) of the devil.**[12]**For we wrestle not against flesh and blood, but against principalities, against powers, against rulers of darkness of this world, against spiritual wickedness in high places.**[13]**Wherefore take**

The "Falling Away"

unto you the whole Amour of God that ye may be able to withstand in the evil day, and having done all to stand.[14] Stand therefore, having your loins girt about with truth, and having on the breastplate of righteousness;[15]And your feet shod with the preparation of the gospel of peace;[16]Above all, taking the shield of faith, wherewith ye shall be able to quench all the fiery darts (homosexuality is one of the darts) of the wicked.[17]And take the helmet of salvation, and the sword of the Spirit, which is the word of God."

If you're practicing homosexuality or feeling enticed to try it, know that you're being influenced by demonic powers. Know that bisexuality and homosexuality is one of the same. It is unnatural, unclean and unacceptable to God. God created man and woman to share holy matrimony and sexual intimacy.

God is the creator of all things including Satan. He ordained Satan to be the **god** of this world. God sent His word and Holy Spirit as protection against the evils of the devil. Therefore, I urge you to seek deliverance from this abominable lifestyle.

RESIST THE DEVIL IN THE NAME OF JESUS, AND HE WILL FLEE.

The "Falling Away"

Chapter Ten
Greed and Jealousy

Greed and jealousy are evil influences that contribute to the increase of hatred, murders, and numerous other crimes.

Ezekiel 22: **"[22]In thee have they taken gifts to shed blood; thou hast taken usury and increase, and thou hast greedily gained of thy neighbors by extortion, and hast forgotten me, saith the Lord God."**

Greed:

In Chapter Five, I briefly mentioned that greed is on the rise and is one of the key factors responsible for corporate failures in our society today. The media has frequently exposed various corporations undergoing criminal investigations because of fraudulent monetary crimes.

Greed and jealousy contributes to the listed below crimes:

- Robbery of banks, individuals, private home invasions, and murders. (Greed/Jealousy)

- Corporations earn huge profits and allocate bonuses to management only - disregarding the supporting staff. (Greed)

- Unjustified salary formulas for employees. The discrepancies of salaries between management and staff are too great. (Greed)

- Decrease of employees' salaries and upper management continues to earn six figure salaries. (Greed)

- Destroying lives by selling illegal drugs. (Greed)

- Multiple taxing of earned income – state and federal taxes are deducted from gross earnings, and purchases from net earnings are taxed. (Greed)

- Retail prices are atrociously higher than wholesale prices especially among designer clothing and accessories that are manufactured inexpensively by minimum wage employees overseas. (Greed)

- False advertisement. Consumers spend millions of dollars on products that don't work. (Greed)

- Telemarketing scam calls offering products that they don't have to obtain your credit card or checking account numbers for fraudulent use. (Greed)

The "Falling Away"

- Pastors having multiple collections of monies in addition to the offering and tithes during Church services. (Greed)

- Some Pastors' hand out envelops to their congregation asking for a specific amount of money in order to receive specific blessings from God. **Note:** God's blessings are free – can't be purchased. (Greed)

- People marrying for material gain or security versus love. (Greed)

- Beneficiaries murdering family member for monetary gain. (Greed/Jealousy)

- Increased cost of housing (rentals/ownership) making it mandatory for most to have roommates. (Greed)

- Increased cost of living is almost unaffordable for the average household. (Greed)

Jealousy:
God is a jealous God, and He clearly indicates in His word that He's jealous when it comes to mankind worshiping another god. This jealousy is justified because He is our creator.

The "Falling Away"

Psalms 78: "[(58)]They angered him with their high places; they aroused his jealousy with their idols."

Being that man was created in the image of God, we all have a measure of ownership jealousy that is similar to God's. For example, think of how an innocent toddler becomes jealous when the mother shows attention to another toddler. The jealous toddler will hit or push the toddler who's getting the attention.

Since Satan wants to mimic God as much as possible, he influences a dangerous jealousy. Unfortunately, this influence affects everyone to some extent. Jealousy is seen everywhere. It's in the church, families, schools, workplace and relationships.

Below are a few evil acts that are noticeably increasing in our society and throughout the world today because of jealousy:

- Increased murders among romantically involved couples of all ages (married and single). Whatever happened to breaking up and going separate ways? Today, far too many relationships end in homicide. (Jealousy)

- Racism is comprised of numerous evil entities (e.g., fears, lies, and ignorance). I believe that

112

jealousy is also one of the complexities of racism.

- Loyalty among families and friends are declining because of increased demonic influences. With the existing breakdown of spiritual connection with God and the lack of conscience, it is becoming difficult to have trusting relationships with anyone. (Greed and Jealousy)

Jude 1: **"(11)Woe unto them! for they have gone in the way of Cain, and ran greedily after the error of Balaam for reward, and perished in the gainsaying (to speak against) of Core."**

The above scripture is referring to the evil characteristics of **jealousy** resulting in murder between two brothers, Abel and Cain; and with **greed** that influenced God's prophet, Balaam, to attempt using his gift from God to practice witchcraft for personal wealth.

Adam and Eve's first son, Cain was a farmer and their second son, Abel was a shepherd. When the two brothers presented their gifts to God, God respected Abel's gift, and Cain's gift was not respected. Cain became **angry, jealous,** and killed his brother. (Jealousy)

The "Falling Away"

Note: Jealousy by default gravitates toward anger. Anger by default can bring about physical harm.

King Balak of Moab, located on the side of Jordan by Jericho, sent his **sorcerers** to ask Balaam, a **prophet of God,** to come to Moab for the purpose of cursing Israel. He offered Balaam much wealth to perform a witchcraft curse. Balaam, knowing that he could only speak the words that God put into his mouth, agreed to go if the King would give him his house filled with gold and silver. (Greed)

For wealth (Greed), Balaam put himself in an uncertain disposition with God who became angry with him. Each time Balaam went to God about Israel, God would bless Israel instead of curse the land. This made King Balak angry, and he made Balaam leave Moab.

In essence, Balaam wanted to use his gift of prophecy from God as witchcraft to curse Israel for the purpose of gaining personal wealth. Today, there are many Balaams in the world. Some Christians are using their spiritual gifts in witchcraft practices for monetary gain. In these instances, Satan has blinded them to think they're of God when they're of the devil. One must be very careful when using spiritual gifts not to cross the line of evil and good. Witchcraft workers are in danger of God's wrath.

Matthew 7: "**(21)Not everyone who says to me, 'Lord, Lord,' shall enter the kingdom of heaven, but he who does the will of my Father who is in heaven. (22)On that day many will say to me, 'Lord, Lord, did we not prophesy in your name, and cast out demons in your name, and do many mighty works in your name?' (23) And then will I declare to them, 'I never knew you; depart from me, you evildoers.**"

Greed and jealousy are evil. If you are battling with one of these characteristics, ask God to help you to overcome the problem. Each day thereafter, thank God for delivering you from whatever sin that has a hold over your spirit until you're no longer bound. The word says that we already have Victory. Therefore, claim Victory (deliverance) before you see it.

I Corinthians 15: "**(57)But thanks be to God, which giveth us the victory through our Lord Jesus Christ.**"

The "Falling Away"

Chapter Eleven
Closing Comments

Now that you've read about the increased characteristics that encompass the **"Falling Away,"** some of you may have recognize yourself in some of the portrayals of disobedience and will change your lives because of your newfound awareness. The truth was rejected by many people when Jesus Christ was here ministering and performing miracles. I expect there will be readers who will be in disagreement with some of the explanations given regarding evils that are afflicting people throughout the world. Some readers will not accept the truth because they are spiritually disconnected from God and cannot hear or see with their spiritual ears and eyes, or because they're trapped in a self-righteous or religious state-of-mind.

There will be readers who, at this time, are not ready to let go of their disobedient lifestyles and accept Christ as their Savior. However, their names are already written in the **"Book of Life"** because sometime in the future they're going to accept Christ and let go of their sins. Perhaps this book will be influential towards them making that important decision of acceptance.

The "Falling Away"

God, the omnipotent, knew before the creation of this world who would be born into it and who would accept Him. Therefore, everyone who accepts Christ as Savior, names are already in the **"Book of Life."**

Below scriptures is confirmation of the **"Book of Life"**:

<u>Revelation 17</u>: **"[8]The beast that you saw was, and is not, and is to ascend from the bottomless pit and go to perdition; and the dwellers on earth whose names have not been written in the book of life from the foundation of the world, will marvel to behold the beast, because it was and is not and is to come."**

<u>Revelation 20</u>: **"[12]And I saw the dead, great and small, standing before the throne, and books were opened. Also another book was opened, which is** the book of life. And the dead were judged by wha**t was written in the books, by what they had done."**

<u>Revelation 20</u>: **<u>"[15]And if any one's name was not found written in the book of life, he was thrown into the lake of fire</u>."**

Biblical scriptures were included to support the validity of what I've written. Therefore, if you have doubt or cannot comprehend the scriptures, ask God to reveal to you the truth. He does not discriminate. When you call on Him – He'll answer. Just as He speaks to me, He'll speak to you. Tomorrow isn't promised to any of us. We had nothing to do with coming into this world; and, we will not have control over when it is time to go to the spiritual world. A wise man prepares for his future here on earth and for the eternal life that is to follow. An unwise man thinks of such as being foolishness. We all are running out of time here on earth and need to give serious thoughts about our eternal spiritual life that follows.

Metaphorically speaking, this life is a temporary journey. We are living a life based on what we've learned. If you pass the test by learning and doing the right things, you're on your way to heaven. If you have not learned the truth and are doing everything wrong, then you're on your way to hell/hades, a place that is tormenting and where the fire never quenches. Both places do exist.

There was a time in my life when I was self-righteous and a traditional believer. I went to Church on Sundays, was a lead singer in the choir, and didn't know very much about God's word. Therefore, I leaned on my own understanding as to what I considered to be acceptable and unacceptable to God. Had anyone told me then that I was on my way to hell, I would not have believed it. Satan had me thinking, while living disobediently, that I was right with God and was on the straight and narrow path to heaven. I was skeptical of people with spiritual gifts because I lacked knowledge pertaining to them. I had always imagined God as being far away, and thought since there were so many people in the world, that it was impossible for Him to know each time I sinned. My carnal mind could not comprehend the overall omnipotence of God. I was spiritually disconnected from Him.

One morning, I took a prescribed medication that caused my heart to stop. I went to bed at 10:00 a.m. and woke up the next morning around the same time. During the 24 hours after taking the medicine, every vital organ in my body was deteriorating at a rapid pace. My muscles, including the heart, nerves, and my blood cells became severely abnormal. My heart stopped, and I died.

While my spirit was out of the body, I remember frequently looking at myself lying in the bed and touching the new wallpaper that I had just hung on my bedroom walls. It never occurred to me that I was dead. What a life changing experience. My spirit never left my bedroom; and I didn't go through a tunnel like many have spoken about when they died. My last memory was when I re-entered my physical body. From this experience, I learned that when you first die, you're not aware that you are out of your physical body (dead), and you don't depart from this world immediately. When I woke up, my legs were paralyzed from the knees down. **This was the first miracle that took place in my new life. God raised me from the dead**.

After the doctor examined me, he said that it was a miracle that I was alive and probably would not survive. I had been given approximately three days to live, and could not imagine dying again. I was afraid, and kept hearing a voice in my thoughts repeating over and over, **"I've got you now. You're going to die and go to hell."** Having never heard that voice before, I somehow knew that it was Satan. There was another voice speaking to my thoughts that said, **"Put your trust in me and not in man thus saith the Lord."** God identified himself.

The second day of hospitalization, my sister anointed me with olive oil in the name of Jesus. As she prayed and layed hands on me to receive healing, gigantic invisible hands went around my waist and lifted me from the bed. I rushed out of the hospital room down the corridors thanking God. I was walking on paralyzed legs. While walking, I felt huge invisible hands holding me tightly and carrying me. My feet were touching the floor, yet I felt as though I was floating. The nurses who had been bathing me were in tears.

The "Falling Away"

They knew I was unable to walk and that a miracle was taking place. **This was the second miracle in my new life.**

God revealed himself to me in a way that is uncommon to many. He had an angel come to my sick bed, lift me to my feet, and carry me down the hospital corridor for others to witness the miracle. The next day, God began speaking to me. I could hear Him in my thoughts. He gave me healing scriptures and told me where to find them in the Bible. He taught me how to use His word as a weapon against sickness. What an awesome God. I had never imagined Him to be so real. He is the same today as He was yesterday.

After the walking miracle took place, my body began to improve each day. I remained in the hospital for one month. Prior to leaving the hospital, my doctors told me that I would never fully recuperate from the damage that had occurred. I knew, by faith, that God had already healed me because His word said so **(Isaiah 53:5 and I Peter 2:24)**. I knew I had to believe that I was healed regardless of the abnormal symptoms and pain that existed in my body. I refused to claim what was physically wrong and continued to confess that I was healed until every part of my body became completely normal.

The "Falling Away"

Isaiah 53: "[5]But he was wounded for our transgressions, he was bruised for our iniquities; upon him was the chastisement that made us whole, and <u>with his stripes we are healed</u>."

I Peter 2: "[24]He himself bore our sins in his body on the tree, that we might die to sin and live to righteousness. By his wounds you have been healed."

There was no medicine that could heal my body. Six months later, after using God's word as medicine and as a weapon like the Lord instructed me to do, my body became completely healed. The heart condition that I was afflicted with since childhood no longer existed.

God restored my body organs, and my ability to walk. **<u>This was the third miracle in my new life.</u>**

Prior to finding God, I had been searching for something and didn't know what it was that I was looking for. **No one** or **any material possession** could satisfy this longing that I had. I could not let anyone get too close and pursued many challenging careers seeking happiness – nothing truly gave me happiness or peace. This tragic experience was the best thing that ever happened to me. It was a blessing in disguise, and I give the praise to God.

The "Falling Away"

The first several years after God revealed himself to me, I made it my priority to learn as much as I could about His word. Having a curious nature, I searched scriptures on every subject of interest. Of course, the first research I did was about angels. After all, I was touched and carried by an angel. I wanted to know what God thoughts were pertaining to what I could do and not do as a Christian. After going to church for many years and knowing so little about God, I realized that I could not afford to rely on traditional teachings. Therefore, I asked God to anoint me with His understanding and wisdom of His word, and He did just that.

Today, after many years of studying God's word, He has recreated my life to be pleasing to Him. I have an unshakable peace within something I didn't have prior to getting to know Him. I, often times, speak to God out loud, and He answers through my thoughts or will lead me to the appropriate scripture. The more I study the word, my outlook about life and people changes. He has removed old baggage (mental/spiritual hang ups) that had me bound. He has given me the confidence to achieve whatever I believe and desire. He has opened my spiritual ears and eyes to discern circumstances. He has filled me with His love, and crowned me with His favor. Now, I know who I am, where I'm headed, and what I want.

My prior disobedient life was exciting, adventurous and empty. The thought of becoming a disciplined Christian was a turn off to me. To my surprise, I was wrong. When you're not entangled in bondage with man-made religious traditions and self-righteousness, Christianity is the most powerful and exciting life one can live. In comparing the two lifestyles, there is no comparison. I would not change being a child of God for anyone or anything.

If you're not ready to accept Christ as your personal savior, it is the same as saying you're not ready for life. **For to live without Christ, you're already spiritually dead according to the Bible.** Living on the broad pathway, **living in disobedience** to God's laws, is the direction to hell, **STOP**. Change your direction to the straight and narrow path that leads to heaven. Tomorrow isn't promised, and gambling with your life can result in eternal torment.

Remember that Jesus Christ was crucified and shed his blood for **all** of us, even those who crucified Him. Remember, there is no sin that the power of His **REDEEMPTIVE BLOOD** can't deliver one from.

I John 1: "[7]**But if we walk in the light, as he is in the light, we have fellowship one with**

The "Falling Away"

another, and the blood of Jesus Christ his Son cleanseth us from all sin."

Hebrews 4: "[13]Nothing in all creation is hidden from God's sight. Everything is uncovered and laid bare before the eyes of Him to whom we must give account."

John 3: "[16]For God so loved the world that He gave His only begotten Son, that whosoever believeth in Him should not perish, but have everlasting life."

Colossians 1: "[12]Giving thanks unto the Father, which hath made us meet to be partakers of the inheritance of the saints in light: [13]Who hath delivered us from the power of darkness, and hath translated us into the kingdom of his dear Son: [14]In whom we have redemption through his blood, even the forgiveness of sins: [15]Who is the image of the invisible God, the firstborn of every creature: [16])For by him were all things created, that are in heaven, and that are in earth, visible and invisible, whether they be thrones, or dominions, or principalities, or powers: all things were created by him, and for him: [17]And He is before all things, and by Him all things consist. [18]And he is the head of the body, the church: who is the beginning, the

The "Falling Away"

firstborn from the dead; that in all things he might have the preeminence."

SALVATION IS FREE because Christ has already paid the price.

You can pray right now and ask God to come into your heart and receive the new birth. Simply talk to Him as you would talk to your friend. You might want to pray a prayer similar to this:

God, I don't know you personally, but I want to know you. I believe that Jesus Christ is the Son of God, and that he died in order that I might be saved. I repent for the disobedient lifestyle that I've been living. I don't want to go to hell. I ask that you come into my heart and cleanse me, fill me with your love and Holy Spirit who will give me the power to overcome and defeat Satan and his influences. I ask and believe in the name of Jesus Christ. Amen

After praying the above prayer of repentance and asking God to come into your heart, you must believe. This is what makes it happen. It's called FAITH. In order to grow in God, you need to do the following on a regular basis:

    a) Study God's word daily,
    b) Pray to God daily,

126

The "Falling Away"

    c) Seek water baptism and fellowship with other believers, and

    d) Keep your heart pure daily by rebuking those thoughts that are not of God.

Satan will become angry because you have accepted the Lord, and he will try to convince you to hold on to your sinful life. He will lie to you and tell you that you're not saved. Rebuke him, in the name of Jesus, and tell him that he's a liar.

A new reborn Christian doesn't change over night. The transformation comes as we become closer to God. In learning how to walk the "straight and narrow," consider your self a baby in Christ because that's what you are. Know that you are going to fall into sin and do some of the old things of the past. When this happens, you're not going to feel good about it because God's chastisement is at work. Don't condemn yourself because of falling, just get up, repent, and keep going. We sin less as we get to know the Lord. Remember, Christians are tempted in the same manner that others are, and none are perfect. God blessed us with the privilege of "repenting" because He's aware of our shortcomings. After all, sinners don't repent because sin is their way of doing things.

I conclude by saying that this is a serious prophetic time that the world is currently experiencing. People have turned away from the truth of God. They're doing their own thing. The Church is guilty of the same by **allowing greed, compromising God's word, lack of His anointing power (Holy Ghost), and reproof of sins** to exist within the "Houses of Worship." The majority of today's Christians are very much like the Pharisees, self-righteous (lukewarm). Perhaps this is why God says there will be few who find the way.

The **"Falling Away"** is upon us. Look around and see for yourself.

I pray that God's anointing and blessings shower upon every reader of this book.

The "Falling Away"

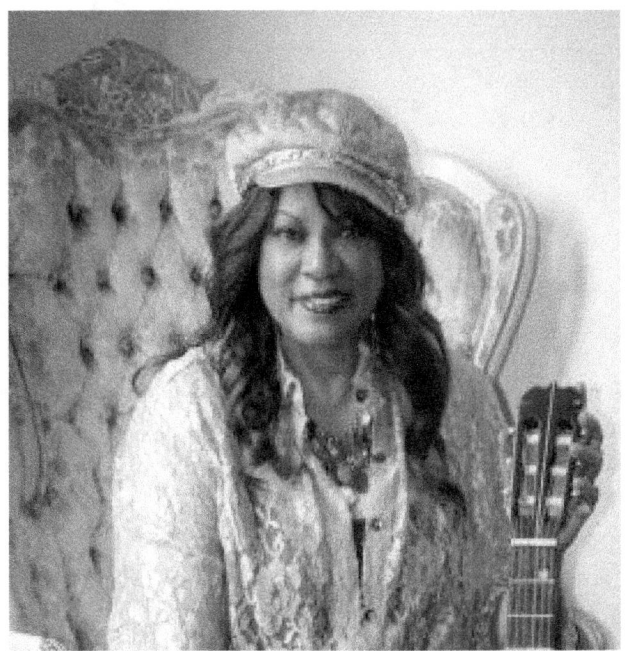

THERESA A. FULLER, AUTHOR